D0568828

Along
Martin Luther King

Along
Martin Luther King

TRAVELS ON BLACK AMERICA'S MAIN STREET

Jonathan Tilove

Photographs by Michael Falco

Random House • New York

Portions of this work were originally published in the Newhouse News Service
Special Reprint entitled "Along Martin Luther King: A Passage to Black America,"
which appeared in various newspapers in 2002.

Permissions acknowledgments can be found on page 205.

LIBRARY OF CONGRESS CATALOGING-IN-PUBLICATION DATA
Tilove, Jonathan.
Along Martin Luther King: travels on black America's main street / by Jonathan
Tilove; photographs by Michael Falco.
p.   cm.
ISBN 1-4000-6080-X
1. African Americans—History—1964– 2. African Americans—Social conditions—
1975– 3. African Americans—Social life and customs. 4. African American
neighborhoods. 5. King, Martin Luther, Jr., 1929–1968—Influence. 6. Street
names—United States. 7. Streets—United States—Pictorial works. 8. United
States—Description and travel. 9. United States—History, Local. 10. United
States—History, Local—Pictorial works. I. Falco, Michael. II. Title.

E185.615.T576 2003
973'.0496073—dc21   2003046610

Random House website address: www.atrandom.com

Printed in the United States of America on acid-free paper

9 8 7 6 5 4 3 2 1

First Edition

Book design by Mercedes Everett

To my wife, Jo-Ann Moriarty, and children, Dylan and Aria, for their love and understanding.

To the memory of Robert and Martha Tilove, wonderful parents and ennobling human beings.

And to Marion Tumbleweed Beach, who knows more than anyone I've ever met, with the possible exception of my uncle Gus.

J.T.

Nothing is ever the same as they said it was. It's what I've never seen before that I recognize.

— Diane Arbus

Foreword

A Cultural Love Song
Haki R. Madhubuti

Along Martin Luther King is a wonderful and appropriate gift to the memory, work, ministry, and commitment of Dr. Martin Luther King, Jr., and the movement he led, inspired, and for which, finally, he died. This tribute by Jonathan Tilove, with photographs by Michael Falco, published in the fortieth anniversary year of the historic march on Washington and King's visionary "I Have a Dream" speech, only enlarges the seminal and singular significance of Dr. King.

The idea for a book about traveling many of the nation's Martin Luther King streets—650 of them, traversing urban and rural cities, towns, and villages from down south to up south, from Harlem to Oakland—is nothing less than brilliant. With insight and integrity, Tilove skillfully writes an untold story waiting to be discovered.

There is a road that winds its way through the heart and soul of black America. It may be called a boulevard, a drive, an avenue, a street, or a way, but it is always named Martin Luther King. It happened without grand design but with profound, if unrecognized, consequences. . . . Map them and you map a nation within a nation, a place where white America seldom goes and black America can be itself. It is a parallel universe with a different center of gravity and distinctive sensibilities. . . . There is no other street like it.

This was an imposing undertaking, leading Octavius Miller of Portland, Oregon, to state, "You guys must be on some kind of spiritual journey." Indeed, if it is not spiritual, most certainly it is soul- and mind-altering. If one wants to understand a people and their culture, one must travel into their interior. Martin Luther King streets mark the epicenter of most black communities in America. Only streets named after Marcus Garvey and Malcolm X are certain to be located on the black side of town. However, unlike Garvey and Malcolm, King was able to link the many gradations of black thought, activism, politics, faith, lifestyles, and classes into an effective force for progressive and revolutionary change.

It is obvious that Tilove and Falco represent a new generation of witness and chronicler. The strength of this book resides in the author's and the photographer's ability to listen, observe, document, and create. There are many revelations here, and it is clear that, as outsiders, they had to earn the trust and respect of black folks across this land. I do not find it unusual that they were able to do so. Black people remain a people with open hearts; it is a condition and survival strategy that Martin Luther King lived by, and that he taught us to live by.

The generosity of the people who shared their stories, and Tilove's talent in weaving them into an interesting and compelling narrative as he complements the powerful photographs of Falco, defines the uniqueness and originality of this book. The stories of these streets are intimate and timeless. They are modern-day love songs waiting to be told.

Jonathan Tilove writes, "What unites the black nation along King is a shared terrain, a sense of place and predicament. After that, anything goes. About the only thing that all black folk in America have in common is contending with being black in America, figuring out what it means to be black in America. That turns out to be enough. That turns out to be plenty." It's an engaging and perceptive statement from an outsider.

Where else but along Martin Luther King would you find Zora Neale Hurston, Jaramogi Abebe Agyeman and the Shrine of the Black Madonna, Lu Palmer, Chokwe Lumumba, Marion Tumbleweed Beach, Juneteenth, black music, Julian Richardson and Marcus Books, Griffin Funeral Home, Walter Mosley, Charles Tisdale, Morris Brown College, Robert Moses and the Algebra Project, J. Richard Harris, Floyd Caldwell, black churches of all denominations, the Third World Press, poet Jolivette Anderson, and the common folks who populate Selma, Galveston, Chicago, Houston, Belle Glade, Jasper, Detroit, Oakland, and all points in between that, like Harlem, have "history on every corner."

This book is an extraordinary journey. There are smiles on each page. Tilove and Falco document the geography of a people on a street whose inhabitants feel free enough to speak truth from their souls. Tilove accurately notes that whites are lost on MLK and blacks are found. The street is blackly defined: "The map of King streets, like the map of black America it so tenaciously tracks, is the geopolitical synthesis of black insistence and white resistance. Martin Luther King streets don't go, can't go, where they are not wanted."

Along Martin Luther King is cultural nutrition for the unenlightened yet hungry reader. The uniqueness, complexity, and beauty of black people swim throughout the pages. After closely reading the text and studying the photographs I realized that what we really have here is an unselfish and unambiguous act of caring and, possibly, love. Walking, sharing, and sleeping in the black community has a way of transforming most doubters. It brings out the best. Martin Luther King's name is a telegraph. His name tells us who you are, where you come from, where you are going, and who is going with you; his name is legitimization of the past, confirmation of the present, and direction for the future. Jonathan Tilove writes it best:

The genius of King streets is how they honor Martin Luther King in precisely the way the national holiday cannot, by provoking passions and controversy and conflict, by stirring fervent debate about the meaning of life and what kind of street would do him credit. They hit people, quite literally, where they live, where they work. And by laying bare the racial fault lines in one community after another, by calling attention to the circumstances of life in the heart of the black community while demanding better, the streets that bear his name are Martin Luther King's greatest living memorial. They stir, they disturb, they tell the truth, and most miraculously for us, decades after his death, at the turn of a new century, King's streets guide two strangers to the glory of his people. Nice.

Haki R. Madhubuti
poet, Distinguished University Professor,
and director of the MFA program in creative
writing at Chicago State University

Contents

Introduction

For various reasons, the average, struggling, non-morbid Negro
is the best-kept secret in America. His revelation to the public is
the thing needed to do away with that feeling of difference
which inspires fear, and which ever expresses itself in dislike.

Zora Neale Hurston,
"What White Publishers Won't Print,"
Negro Digest, April 1950

The idea for the journey on which this book is based took root in the Mississippi Delta. The year was 1994. I had been writing about race for Newhouse News Service since 1991, and I was traveling the Delta for a story about what had changed in the thirty years since Freedom Summer, and what had not. I was struck as I traveled from one town to another that when I would stop to ask directions to some destination on the black side of town, the answer would sound back with the sameness of a blues refrain: "Just head on down to Martin Luther King."

I was familiar with streets being named for Martin Luther King around the country, but not until that trip to Mississippi did I realize just what a phenomenon it was. Even black neighborhoods that did not appear to have a lot else to show for the civil rights revolution had their street named for MLK. Often it seemed to be the main street through the black community, steeped in history and a relic of what for these black business districts were the better days of Jim Crow.

Canton, Mississippi

A sign is born. Public Services workshop, Belle Glade, Florida.

I imagined trying to trek across America connecting the dots from one Martin Luther King street to the next. I wondered where a journey along Martin Luther King would lead. I knew it was a great idea but, to be done even half right, an ambitious one.

It was not until five years later, in the fall of 1999, that I took the idea to the street. I was back in Mississippi, at Lanier High School in Jackson, to do a story about the intriguing circumstance that both Robert Moses, a prime architect of Freedom Summer, and Ouida Atkins, the daughter of Ross Barnett, the segregationist governor who had played Pharaoh to Moses' Moses back then, were teaching at the same all-black high school. Lanier is located on Jackson's Martin Luther King Drive. I was working for the first time with Mike Falco, a freelance photographer from New York, and the plan was for us to spend some time on the street and see what came of it.

And that was it.

Choose the metaphor you like—down the rabbit hole, through the looking glass, out the door of your Kansas home now plunked down in the middle of Oz—but almost as soon as we set foot on Martin Luther King it seemed like we had entered another world, another dimension, ever there but never, to the stranger, apparent. In the abstract, I hadn't known whether this idea of journeying along streets named for King might not sound like a bit of conceit—better in theory than in practice. But once we were on the street, it seemed to make perfect sense, to us and to those we encountered.

And from that first day we found ourselves encountering some remarkable people.

The men playing pool checkers in front of Brown's Freeway Service Station on MLK, each and every one, bore quietly lyrical witness to their first-person sagas of crossing Mississippi's River Jordan. Jessica Drummer, one of Ouida

The Dr. is in. Willie B. McKenzie replaces an old Martin Luther King Jr. Boulevard sign with a new one, adding "Dr." before the name, January 2003.

Atkins's students, brought us back to her home on MLK and the welcoming warmth of her mother, Beola, and the rest of the Drummer family. The Malcolm X Grassroots Center next to Lanier High School led us to Chokwe Lumumba, the revolutionary nationalist attorney who had moved south as part of the Republic of New Afrika, a radical movement that is rarely acknowledged in mainstream accounts of the black freedom struggle. I assumed he would view us with suspicion, at least. If he did, he did not show it. We talked for a couple of hours, mostly about the center's youth basketball program, he posed for photos, and we returned a year and a half later for his annual Black History Classic basketball tournament.

Mike and I left Mississippi excited, convinced that we were onto something great. And fortunately, after this trip and every succeeding one, we had Mike's photographs to prove that our enthusiasm, bordering on rapture, was not based on some hallucinated experience. It was real, it was vivid, and it could to some degree be transmitted to others.

Shortly after our trip to Mississippi I traveled to Stanford University for a conference on race, and while I was there spent some time exploring the Martin Luther King Way in nearby Oakland. When I wandered into the Indigo Shack, an African arts shop on MLK, I introduced myself to the owner, Shawna Holbrook, and explained what I was doing. I mentioned having just visited the MLK in Jackson, Mississippi. Holbrook said she knew all about that street, her grandmother lived just off it, she used to spend summers there and still took turns, along with other members of her family now scattered across the country, returning home there to spend time with Grandma.

"Same street," I said. Same street, I thought, with the chill of epiphany. It seems so obvious now, but the notion that these streets were connected, one to another, across America, like family, felt like a revelation that could serve as a guiding theme for our travels along King.

We began our journey in earnest on Martin Luther King Day 2000 in Belle Glade, Florida, a place picked precisely for being so far off the beaten track, to test the thesis that these streets were indeed connected one to the next.

We chose our other destinations to include both places that were important

Selma, Alabama

touchstones of the black experience—Harlem, Chicago, Atlanta, Oakland—and a cross section of streets by size and location. We timed our visits to coincide, when possible, with moments, events, occasions that cumulatively would expose us to the widest range of life along these streets. And we let the streets themselves direct us.

In Belle Glade we learned about Morris Brown, a historically black college on MLK in Atlanta, and arranged to spend Freshman Week there in August 2000. On returning from Atlanta, we heard that the upcoming mayoral runoff election in Selma—a pivot point of King's struggle—might well lead to the election of that symbolically supercharged little city's first black mayor, so we headed to the MLK there for the last days before the vote.

We wanted to be on an MLK for the 2000 presidential election, and figured that no city takes its politics more seriously than Chicago. Direct from Chicago we headed back to Belle Glade to see Glades Central (which produces more pro-

Retired Martin Luther King Jr. Boulevard signs, Belle Glade, Florida

fessional football players than any high school in America) in the annual Muck Bowl, and wound up in the eye of the storm surrounding the disputed Florida vote (Belle Glade is in Palm Beach County). A few weeks later it was back to Chicago for the wake and funeral of the poet Gwendolyn Brooks and, after the cemetery, a repast at Chicago State University on King, where she had taught.

For King Day 2001, and on many occasions since, we were on 125th Street, the MLK in Harlem, the most famous black street in the world. In April 2001 we returned to Jackson for Chokwe Lumumba's Black History Classic and, it turned out, Jessica Drummer's Lanier High School prom. In May 2001 we returned to the MLK Way in Oakland, a city getting less black by the day, and from there traveled up the West Coast to the MLK in Portland, Oregon, to get the feel of a King street in a much whiter place and contending with the forces of gentrification.

Beginning Juneteenth 2001 on the MLK in Galveston, Texas, where that celebration of late word of emancipation started, we sought to capture our original impulse to connect the dots from one King to another in quick succession and introduce the rhythms of a road trip into our journey: two weeks, five states, nineteen MLKs (six states and twenty MLKs if you count our ending the trip by flying back to New York for an anniversary celebration of the McCollough Sons of Thunder shout band at the United House of Prayer for All People on the MLK in Harlem).

Our Juneteenth road trip, zigzagging eleven hundred miles up the nation's midsection, was an exhilarating ride, despite following the rough outline of a macabre itinerary I had worked up to test the limits of irony: stops on the MLKs in Huntsville, Texas, the prison and execution capital of Texas, and just up the road, in Livingston, home to the Texas death row. Sunday worship at the church on MLK in Jasper, Texas, where they held the funeral for James Byrd, Jr., who was walking along that MLK when he accepted the ride from the men who tied

San Augustine, Texas

him to the back of their pickup truck and dragged him to his death. A visit to the Mabel Bassett Correctional Center, a maximum-security women's prison on MLK in Oklahoma City, from which Wanda Jean Allen was taken that January to be executed, the first black woman to be put to death in America in half a century. And, as our final destination, the MLK in Leavenworth, Kansas, not far from the military death row where a black army private, Dwight Loving, waits to become the first soldier executed since 1961.

We also followed King streets, and those we met along them, to other places they might lead us. Clyde Lister, whom we met at Hicks Mortuary on the MLK in Center, Texas, guided us to the dirt-road community of Africa, Texas, where he lives. The poet Jolivette Anderson, whom we met at Lanier on the MLK in Jackson, led us much later to the beach at Coney Island for a ceremony of remembrance for the lives lost in the Middle Passage, and then to an annual gathering of the Five Percent Nation in Harlem, two blocks north of the MLK there.

We would generally spend about a week on a street, and sometimes make return visits. I would usually go a couple of days ahead of Mike to get the lay of the land. The visits were mixes of careful planning and serendipity. The preparation involved getting to know something about the street, its history, and what was on it, before we got there, and figuring out the best time to go. Sometimes we did some arranging ahead of time when just showing up unannounced or on short notice might not work. We got permission from Dolores Cross, the president of Morris Brown, to spend Freshman Week there. We arranged a tour of Mabel Bassett, the women's prison in Oklahoma City. We made an appointment to see Haki R. Madhubuti, the Chicago poet and publisher, whose schedule would require advance notice.

But once on the street, we went with the flow, and most of what we found on our journey we encountered for the first time walking or riding along King. Serendipity was the rule and, it sometimes seemed, very nearly our religion.

Leaving the harsh midday sun of the MLK in Texarkana and a short time later entering what seemed the instantly more forgiving landscape of Oklahoma, Mike said he had been envisioning photographing a black cowboy on King.

"Yeah, that would be good," I said. Good luck, I thought. But at our very next stop, as we pulled up on the MLK in the town of Idabel, there before our eyes were horses grazing on acres of green pasture. Within minutes Mike had met the serene black man, Andrew Young, who owned the land, the horses, and some steers elsewhere yet insisted he was not a cowboy but a "country boy," a designation he felt suggested greater versatility.

Harlem, New York

Nearly a year earlier, back in Washington and checking out the possibilities of a visit to Oklahoma City, I had come upon a listing for the Miss Black Oklahoma pageant on MLK. I tried calling, left messages, but never heard back. But no sooner had we arrived at the Zodiac Motorcycle Club on Oklahoma City's King than we were told that the Miss Black Oklahoma contestants were preparing for Saturday night's pageant at an old hotel just down MLK.

At Yam Yam's Southern Barbecue on the MLK in Portland, Oregon, we met Octavius Miller, a music promoter, who the next night had us on his radio show. "You guys must be on some kind of spiritual journey," Miller said. I don't know. I'm not a particularly spiritual person. But there did seem to be something more than just good fortune guiding us on what came to feel like a mission, joyful and profound.

Before each trip on King I would despair that this time it wouldn't happen again, that we would arrive on the street and find ourselves becalmed, our momentum stalled, whatever force had been guiding us gone. That never happened. But then, of course, that was because we were not, after all, transmigrating to Wonderland or Oz. What we had stumbled upon was not a phantasm, a projection, or a fluke. It was, simply, black America, arrayed along its Main Street, even if it looked a bit different from what all the contributors to the popular imagination would have it. It was, as Zora Neale Hurston put it half a century before, "the best-kept secret in America." Fantastic but true. I swear. I was there.

Along
Martin Luther King

Chapter 1

The Main Street

"Every town got a Martin Luther King."

Annie Williams, Sudsy City Laundromat,
Martin Luther King Jr. Boulevard,
Belle Glade, Florida, 2000

There is a road that wends its way through the heart and soul of black America. It may be called a boulevard, a drive, an avenue, a street, or a way, but it is always named Martin Luther King.

It happened without grand design but with profound, if unrecognized, consequences. Together, the circumstance of segregation, the martyrdom that made Martin Luther King the every-hero of a people, and the countless separate struggles to honor him have combined to create a black Main Street from coast to coast.

Some 650 streets are named for King in cities and towns from one end of the country to the other, with more added every year and no end in sight. Map them and you map a nation within a nation, a place where white America seldom goes and black America can be itself. It is a parallel universe with a different center of gravity and distinctive sensibilities, kinship at two or three degrees of separation, not six.

There is no other street like it.

Dock Jackson crossing the freshly minted Martin Luther King Boulevard in Elgin, Texas

Glades Central High School marching band, Martin Luther King Day, Belle Glade, Florida

Over the course of two years, a reporter and a photographer traveled along Martin Luther King streets of every size and description. Our only mission was to see where a journey along these streets of a single name would lead. We discovered that it leads everywhere—to every facet of black life, politics, thought, faith, culture, history, and experience—that in remarkable and uncanny ways it burrows deep into the marrow of that which is black America and into the enduring meaning of King's life.

Along the way, there are barber and beauty shops, fast-food chicken franchises and slow-cooked barbecue joints with sweet iced tea and standing fans. There are the brilliantly colored murals paying homage to Martin, Malcolm, Rosa, Billie, Biggie, and Tupac. There are churches of every size, denomination, and shade of Jesus, more preachers than pulpits, black Muslims spanning the cosmological continuum, and in Galveston, Texas, a Korean War veteran scaling

Marion Favors, Blood-N-Fire Ministries homeless shelter, Martin Luther King Drive, Atlanta

a four-foot fish in front of a gigantic turquoise Buddha he salvaged from a Mardi Gras parade.

There is, in both Harlem and Dallas, the intersection of MLK and Malcolm X; in Selma, the intersection of MLK and Jeff Davis; and in just about the middle of nowhere, East Texas, the corner of MLK and MLK. There are poets, players, writers, rappers, thinkers, tinkers, strutters, shouters, and with inspiring regularity, local heroes who, without pomp or portfolio, in one mortal guise or another, keep the spirit of King on King. And everywhere there is endless, ardent talk about what it means to be African in America.

Stretches of many King streets have a ragged, wasted quality to them. The comedian Chris Rock famously advised, "If a friend calls you on the telephone and says they're lost on Martin Luther King Boulevard and they want to know what they should do, the best response is 'Run!' " It has become a commonplace

Chasity Shears at First Baptist Church, Martin Luther King Street, Selma, Alabama

of popular culture to identify a Martin Luther King street as a generic marker of black space and, not incidentally, of ruin, as a sad and ironic signpost of danger, failure, and decline, and as a rueful rebuke of a people's preoccupation with symbolic victories over actual progress.

But pause on King, begin talking to folks, and the clutter, the noise of the rest of America falls away, and you are transported beyond the sometimes battered facade into a black America that, with astonishing welcome, reveals itself as not only more separate and self-contained than imagined but also more tightly interconnected, more powerfully whole. Many black people have moved beyond the neighborhoods through which King runs (though there are now

Freshman Week at Morris Brown College, Martin Luther King Drive, Atlanta

King streets in new black suburbs), but few live beyond the reach of the sounds, sentiments, and stories rooted on King. These are streets united by struggle and circumstance, by history and happenstance. One King street leads to the next and next and back again.

For many whites, a street sign that says Martin Luther King tells them they are lost. For many blacks, a street sign that says Martin Luther King tells them they are found.

When Dock Jackson—who played a role in naming the MLK in his home-town of Bastrop, Texas, where he is on the council, and in nearby Elgin, where he is the park director—arrived in Oklahoma City on business and needing a

haircut, he simply headed to Martin Luther King and found Robert Gates's barbershop. When Barber Gates travels to a new place, he does the same. "When I don't know where I'm going, I'll find MLK."

Lives are lived from one King street to the next.

The Reverend Daniel Stafford, pastor of Peaceful Rest Baptist Church on Martin Luther King Boulevard in Jasper, Texas, is also pastor of Starlight Baptist Church on Martin Luther King Drive in De Ridder, Louisiana.

Dolores Cross was president of Chicago State University on King Drive before becoming president of Morris Brown College on Atlanta's King Drive. She grew up in Newark, New Jersey, graduating from Central High School on what is now Martin Luther King Boulevard. When she returned to Newark after the publication of her book, *Breaking Through the Wall: A Marathoner's Story* (published by Chicago State's Haki Madhubuti's Third World Press), she signed copies at St. James AME Church on MLK.

"It's haunting," says Cross.

The NFL linebacker Ray Lewis, who led the Baltimore Ravens to a 2000 conference championship playing on the MLK in Baltimore, was the most valuable player in the Super Bowl played on the MLK in Tampa, and spent the early preseason on trial at the Fulton County Courthouse on the MLK in Atlanta for murders committed in the hours following the previous Super Bowl. Throughout his trial (he ended up pleading guilty to obstruction of justice), his spiritual needs were tended to by the courtside presence of the Reverend J. Richard Harris, a minister we know from the MLK in Belle Glade, Florida.

On a late May day on the MLK in Portland, Oregon, the afternoon light streaming through an open door of a gospel festival at the Miracles Club illumines two little sisters playing with funeral home fans bearing the same sepiawarm image of Martin Luther King we saw on an identical fan eight months earlier in the hands of a laughing young woman sitting on a folding chair at a campaign rally on the MLK in Selma, Alabama. It was at that same rally that we met Martin Luther King III on Martin Luther King, and Emmanuel ben Avra-

Dolores Cross, president of Morris Brown College, Martin Luther King Drive, Atlanta, past president of Chicago State University, Martin Luther King Drive, Chicago

Lanier High School prom, Jackson, Mississippi

ham, the Trenton, New Jersey, community activist (raised Muslim, he later became a Baptist before converting to Orthodox Judaism) who led the effort to name the MLK there and in his native Newark, New Jersey.

On MLK Day 2000 in Belle Glade, Florida, we meet Angela Williams, just moved onto MLK there from Trenton, where she had lived near that city's MLK. "Same damn street," she says. "Think about it. Every Martin Luther King looks the same. The worst street in the city is named after Martin Luther King. Give a black man a black street in a black neighborhood? But that's not the purpose. The purpose is to honor him. They should name Main Street Martin Luther King Boulevard."

But Annie Williams (no relation), who lives and works on Belle Glade's MLK, managing the Sudsy City Laundromat, disagrees. "Martin Luther King would not fit on Main because myself, being black, I would like it to run just like it's running through a black town. Got to keep it black, got to keep this black, Martin Luther King got to be black," she says.

It is a debate that can be heard from one MLK to the next, that echoes across America, because, as Annie Williams puts it, "Every town got a Martin Luther King." Or so it seems.

In the decades since King's assassination, the grassroots efforts to name streets for him have gained momentum in the face of substantial inertia and re-

Beach Dance, Middle Passage ceremony, Coney Island, New York

Bus stop, Martin Luther King Drive, Chicago

sistance. It is a movement with no national organization, no national attention, not even self-knowledge that a movement is what it is—as if the transcontinental railroad had been built piecemeal by folks unaware of one another. The only national leader is King, dead now nearly as many years as he lived but still uniquely able to inspire black unity and activism on his behalf.

Occasionally, King streets turn up in unexpected places. There are two MLKs in Utah, in gritty Ogden and a main thoroughfare leading into Salt Lake City, where to the arriving traveler, the Martin Luther King sign first leaps to view breathtakingly framed against the snowcapped Wasatch Mountains. There is a squib of a street in Newcomerstown, Ohio, a bucolic dot on the map midway between Columbus and Wheeling, West Virginia, that was home to Cy Young and Woody Hayes and, on its MLK, the descendants of some black workers brought in from Alabama early in the century to work in the local foundry. In 1969 they petitioned the village council to rename the street for King, and it was done.

Some Minnesotans were apparently so abashed on reading news stories in early 2002 about their state being one of the few without an MLK that by year's end there were three—on the University of Minnesota campus in Morris; in St. Paul, where the state capitol is now on Rev. Dr. Martin Luther King Jr. Boulevard, and in Mankato, where they named a little street with nothing on it but a new National Guard armory for King. (Two days after Christmas an unidentified motorist mowed down both of Mankato's new MLK street signs while

Rainon Wallace on Martin Luther King Drive, Leavenworth, Kansas

shouting racial epithets at some passing children.) Beyond the borders of the United States, there is a Martin Luther King Boulevard in Dakar, Senegal, another MLK Boulevard in the Dutch city of Drachten, and in Tuscany, a Via Martin Luther King in the lovely little spa town of San Giuliano Terme, where Mary Wollstonecraft Shelley wrote *Frankenstein*.

Sometimes there isn't a King street where you might expect it, like Philadelphia. There are the occasional white folks on King. Former president Bill Clinton has his office on 125th Street, also known as MLK, in Harlem. The would-be presidential assassin John Hinckley is confined indefinitely behind the forbidding walls of St. Elizabeth's, the Victorian psychiatric hospital that sprawls on and on along the MLK in Washington, D.C. There are MLKs that run through black neighborhoods and keep going. Morris Brown College is on the MLK in Atlanta, but so is the World of Coca-Cola, and the road dead-ends at the cemetery where Margaret Mitchell is buried.

But, for the most part, King streets are exactly where you would expect to find them—concentrated in black neighborhoods in communities with significant black populations. According to Derek Alderman, a geographer at East Carolina University, who has studied and mapped the naming of streets for King (he has also studied the naming of public schools for King), the densest swath of King streets is in the Deep South, from East Texas to Florida. Mississippi has at least sixty-five King streets, and King's home state of Georgia has at least seventy.

The more King streets there are, the more blacks in communities without one want one. "We're surrounded by communities, some even smaller than ours, not as progressive as we proclaim to be, they all have streets renamed for Martin Luther King," says Bernita Sims, a leader in the most recent of what has been a decade of futile efforts to name a street for King in High Point, North Carolina. "Thomasville has a street, Lexington has a street. Greensboro has a street. Winston-Salem has a street. Hickory has a street."

Most recently, Sims and others, who did not want their MLK confined to the black community—"everybody benefited from that struggle," says Sims—sought to rename College Drive, but they ran into opposition, starting with High Point University, which while its address is not College Drive, considers it

Debra Stewart, client of MLK Beauty Salon, Smithville, Texas

a matter of honor to keep that name for the street that runs alongside the campus. The city rejected renaming College Drive for King in 2001 and again in 2002, after which the city council changed the rules to make it more difficult to rename streets. "The bottom line is they just don't want the street in town," says Sims, who was elected to the council in 2002 and vows the campaign to name a street for King will continue.

Every King street tells a story: Where it begins. Where it ends. What's on it. What's not on it. Who was in favor of renaming the street. Who was against it. Like all the best battles, the struggle to name a street after King is a fight over turf, pride, and power, and often it does not come easy, if it comes at all. It is the story of streets named, streets not named, streets named and then unnamed, streets given the new name while still keeping the old name, and other things named as consolation prizes for streets not being named (in 2001 it was the train station in Toledo, Ohio).

James Moore at Sims Bayou Park, Martin Luther King Boulevard, Houston

Businesses don't like the bother and expense of changing their addresses. There are always some folks devoted to the history and significance of the old name. But in the scores of skirmishes one also catches a glimpse—or an eyeful—of deeper white resistance and, in the intensity of the reaction, a bracing reminder of the real King, the man with edge and meaning, and not simply the dreamy King of grammar-school coloring contests.

Typically the biggest argument over naming a King street is whether the name should stretch beyond the black community and across the tracks—figuratively and many times literally—to the white side of town.

When Mayor Richard Daley and the Board of Aldermen chose to name South Park Way in Chicago King Drive less than four months after King's death—making it probably the first King street of them all—it did not escape notice that, unlike some other major arteries through the city's black South Side, South Park's thirteen miles never leave the South Side.

On the freshly minted MLK in Elgin, Texas, we visit in June 2001, Dock Jackson, the park director, tells us Elgin lagged thirteen years behind the neighboring cities of Bastrop and Smithville, because the proponents in Elgin wanted both the white and black ends of the street to bear King's name. Finally, he said, they settled for the black half alone.

It might have been the same story back in 1975 in Austin—just west of Elgin—were it not for J. J. Seabrook, an elder statesman of the black community, who suffered a fatal heart attack while imploring the city council not to treat King like that. He died and won. Austin's MLK crosses racial lines and borders the state capitol complex.

Bishop Robert T. McGee of Apostolic Church of Deliverance Jesus Name Temple, Martin Luther King Way, Oakland, California

The dedication on King Day 1993 of Martin Luther King Boulevard in Americus, Georgia, came after a year of ugly arguments, threats, protests, and the memorable suggestion by a deputy fire chief that half the street be named for King and the other half for James Earl Ray, King's convicted assassin.

In 1984 the city of Boynton Beach, Florida, named three blocks of road on the black side of the tracks for King, and then in 1995 extended the name across the tracks through a mostly white waterside development called Mangrove Walk. In 2000 a retired white police officer from Long Island, New York, who had bought a town house in Mangrove Walk sought to unname the newer stretch of MLK. "They sandbagged us," he told the Fort Lauderdale *Sun-Sentinel.* "I didn't buy across the railroad [tracks]. All of a sudden the railroad tracks is over here." Elsewhere he quoted Chris Rock on how ghetto King streets are. "So I don't live in the ghetto. Why is the name there?" He despaired that a hypothetical buyer for his town house from Idaho might lose interest when he discovered that he had to take an MLK to get to it.

He eventually relented, but his concerns have a long pedigree. When folks in Chattanooga's black community marched and pleaded with the city to rename Ninth Street for King in 1981, a leading white developer threatened to scuttle construction of a new office building on Ninth if it became MLK. The street was renamed, the building was built, but it, and a companion building that is home to the corporate headquarters for the Krystal hamburger chain, invented for themselves a new address—Union Square. Those buildings are now owned by a real estate developer, Bob Corker, who in 2001 was elected mayor of Chattanooga.

In Belle Glade, Florida, in 1990 Harma Miller, who was on the city commission at the time, said whites wanted the MLK to end before it reached their "beloved Elks Club. I said no, and made a big fuss about it," and in the end, the whole of Avenue E was given the dual designation Martin Luther King and Avenue E. But when the city did some street repairs in 2000 and replaced a few signs, Miller says Avenue E was writ large, and Martin Luther King was writ so small you had to stop and squint to make it out. That fall, when she became the first black mayor with a black majority on the commission, the first thing she did was replace those signs.

In other cities, the fight to name a street for King has been won, and then lost.

With curious symmetry, in 1986 the councils in both San Diego, California, and Harrisburg, Pennsylvania, renamed their Market Streets—major commercial thoroughfares—Martin Luther King Boulevard, only to have citizens force the issue onto the ballot, where the electorate in both cities the following year resoundingly voted to restore the name Market Street. (Both cities have since named smaller streets for King.) Polls indicated that in 1990 voters in Portland, Oregon, would have undone the naming of Martin Luther King Boulevard there had the courts not intervened and canceled the vote.

The day the San Diego City Council voted to let the people decide whether to reverse the council's decision to name Market Street for MLK, the only councilor who had opposed renaming Market to begin with—a white woman—was quoted as lamenting the mounting controversy, "because that was not Dr. Martin Luther King's way. His way was to avoid controversy."

It is remarkable that less than twenty years after his assassination a public official in a major American city could have had such an upside-down understand-

61st and Martin Luther King Way, Oakland, California

ing of King's life, but it is perhaps fitting that her comments came the year after King's birthday was declared a national holiday. The holiday enshrines King as the most honored black man in American history—a symbol for all his people and for all people—but the inevitable price for his canonization as a civic saint has been the bleaching, year by year, of the meaning, the danger, the risk, and the challenge of King's life.

But as one travels the streets that bear his name, the real King is resurrected. At times the journey along King is like a pilgrimage along the stations of the cross for the martyred hero.

In 1958 Martin Luther King was heckled by black nationalists on what is now the MLK in Harlem and the next day, on the same street, stabbed in the chest by a deranged black woman while signing books. He led the 1965 marches in Selma beginning from Brown Chapel on what is now MLK there, and six weeks earlier, Malcolm X, seventeen days before his own death, came to that

A family at Annual Tribute to Our Ancestors of the Middle Passage, Coney Island, New York

same church to express his solidarity with King. Martin Luther King was tear-gassed in 1966 on what is now the MLK in Canton, Mississippi, on the Memphis-to-Jackson march along which Stokely Carmichael, tear-gassed as well, first roused a crowd to chant "Black Power." The mule-drawn caisson carrying King's casket in 1968 rolled along what is now MLK in his hometown of Atlanta, as it passed Morris Brown College, coming within shouting distance of the modest home where King lived and his widow still does. And for many years, Olivet Baptist Church on King Drive in Chicago took its address from its side street because the pastor, now dead, was such a bitter rival of King's in national black Baptist circles.

The two questions most frequently asked by white people about our journey along MLK are "Are there any that are not just in black neighborhoods?" and "Are there any nice ones?"

The answer to the first question is pretty straightforward. There are King streets that extend beyond the black community, but far fewer than there would be were it not for the objections of white people who simply do not want to live, work, or drive on a street named for Martin Luther King. The map of King streets, like the map of black America it so tenaciously tracks, is the geopolitical synthesis of black insistence and white resistance. Martin Luther King streets don't go, can't go, where they are not wanted.

The second question has become more nettlesome as time has gone on. The implication of this question is that the streets might do more honor to King if they were nicer, a point of view expressed even by many black folks on King. But why? If we wanted nice we could have undertaken a journey along Pleasant Street. Gentrification is about making a street "nice." King's life was not.

The genius of King streets is how they honor Martin Luther King in precisely the way the national holiday cannot, by provoking passions and controversy and conflict, by stirring fervent debate about the meaning of his life and what kind of street would do him credit. They hit people, quite literally, where they live, where they work. And by laying bare the racial fault lines in one community after another, by calling attention to the circumstances of life in the heart of the black community while demanding better, the streets that bear his name are Martin Luther King's greatest living memorial. They stir, they disturb, they tell the truth, and most miraculously for us, decades after his death, at the turn of a new century, King's streets guide two strangers to the glory of his people. Nice.

Chapter 2

The Muck

Ground so rich that everything went wild. . . . Wild cane on either side of the road hiding the rest of the world. People wild too.

Zora Neale Hurston,
Their Eyes Were Watching God, 1937

In the beginning, there was Belle Glade.

The place is primordial, elemental, biblical—its light so luminous, its ebony earth so Garden of Eden fertile, its torment by flood and plague so Old Testament, its faith and fortitude in the face of all its trials, Lord, so Jobian, so black.

We wanted to start our journey somewhere unlikely, off the beaten track. We wanted to spend King Day 2000 on a King street that hadn't come too certainly, where celebrating his life was still fresh with effort and shaky with edge. We wanted to see where a rubbled King street in the back of beyond would lead.

"You close your eyes you're going to miss it," James Leonard, a hairstylist at Betty's Beauty Salon on MLK, says in advance of the 2000 Martin Luther King Day parade.

He's right. The most impressive thing about the King Day parade here is that there is one; the next most impressive thing is that there is an MLK down which to march. On first sight, Belle Glade seems to exist in a benighted world before King.

In the beginning. Belle Glade, Florida.

Masons, Martin Luther King Day Parade

Yet, lost as it is amid the sugarcane and snapping gators along the shores of Lake Okeechobee on the edge of the Everglades, Belle Glade is in uncanny ways not behind the times but ahead of them, more bellwether than backwater, as if the seeds of the black experience first take root in the muck—that's what they call the mud-rich soil where things grow like Jack's beanstalk—and only when they flower here are those seeds blown by the four winds across the rest of Africa America. It caught us by surprise, but perhaps it should not have. Things begin in the beginning.

Consider:

• Two months before the 2000 presidential election, black folks in Belle Glade were screaming about a stolen election, the one in which they lost their first-ever black majority on the city commission in a community where blacks outnumber whites by more than three to one. In November 2000, there were nearly enough botched butterfly ballots at the polling places on MLK in Belle Glade alone to make Al Gore president, to change the course of history.

Spectators observe police participation in the Martin Luther King Day Parade.

• The muck doesn't just produce more sugarcane and sweet corn than any other place in the country. Glades Central High School produces more professional football players than any other high school in America—seven playing in the NFL when we visit. Brad Banks, the Iowa quarterback who finished second in the balloting for the Heisman Trophy in 2002, is out of Belle Glade.

OUT OF THE MUCK

As of January 2003, Belle Glade had produced twenty-one athletes who went on to sign with pro teams. All were graduates of Glades Central High School with the exception of the first, Lawrence Chester, who graduated from Lake Shore High School, the black school in Belle Glade, before desegregation. The list includes the name of the player, the year he went pro, and the name of the team or teams he played with. It includes only National Football League teams, with the exception of Wilford Morgan (number 4), who played for the Tampa Bay Bandits of the United States Football League. Affiliations with teams in Canadian or other professional football leagues are not included. This list was compiled by Glades Central's legendary track coach, Willie McDonald, whose son, Ray, is number 6 on the list. Not yet on the list is Belle Glade's Brad Banks, the Iowa quarterback who was the runner-up for the Heisman Trophy in 2002.

1. Lawrence Chester, 1967. Atlanta Falcons, Detroit Lions (graduated from Lake Shore High School, before desegregation)
2. Anthony Williams, 1972. Buffalo Bills
3. Wayne Stanley, 1974. Cleveland Browns
4. Wilford Morgan, 1984. Tampa Bay Bandits (United States Football League)
5. Jessie Hester, 1985. Los Angeles Raiders, Atlanta Falcons, Indianapolis Colts, Los Angeles Rams, St. Louis Rams
6. Ray McDonald, 1986. New England Patriots, Dallas Cowboys
7. Rodney Westin, 1988. Cleveland Browns, Tampa Bay Buccaneers
8. Louis Oliver, 1989. Miami Dolphins, Cincinnati Bengals
9. Willie Snead, 1989. New York Jets, Houston Oilers
10. John Ford, 1989. Detroit Lions, Seattle Seahawks
11. Jimmy Spencer, 1991. Washington Redskins, New Orleans Saints, Cincinnati Bengals, San Diego Chargers, Denver Broncos
12. Daniel Willis, 1995. Tampa Bay Buccaneers
13. Reidel Anthony, 1997. Tampa Bay Buccaneers, Washington Redskins
14. Fred Taylor, 1998. Jacksonville Jaguars
15. Roosevelt Blackmon, 1998. Green Bay Packers, Cincinnati Bengals
16. Nakia Jenkins, 1998. Signed as an undrafted rookie free agent by New York Jets, waived during training camp. 1999: Signed by Jacksonville Jaguars, released during training camp
17. Johnny Rutledge, 1999. Arizona Cardinals

18. Willie Jones, 1999. St. Louis Rams, Kansas City Chiefs
19. Robert Newkirk, 1999. New Orleans Saints, Chicago Bears
20. JaJuan Seider, 2000. San Diego Chargers, released in preseason
21. James Jackson, 2001. Cleveland Browns

• By the mid-1980s, Belle Glade had the highest AIDS rate in America, and for a while the world, prefiguring the crisis to come in black America. In 2002 Belle Glade also became home to the first medical trials to determine which mix of AIDS drugs best help black people.

But this small town has always been a place of epic misfortune.

In 1960 Edward R. Murrow came here to report *Harvest of Shame*, his landmark documentary on the wretched conditions under which migrant workers live, and they are still harvesting shame in Belle Glade today.

In the 1940s it was a syphilis epidemic.

And the single worst day in Belle Glade history was September 16, 1928, when a hurricane whipped Lake Okeechobee (Seminole for "big water") into a tidal wave that washed away at least eighteen hundred lives and perhaps as many as three thousand, a death toll to rival that of September 11, 2001.

More extraordinary than its suffering, though, and as prototypical, is black Belle Glade's staying power. It is not stoic, not a resigned resilience. It is rhapsodic, devotional, a celebration of home place, blood ties, and survival. People love the muck, leave the muck, shake the last bit of muck off their shoes, and return.

James Leonard, the hairstylist, left Belle Glade when he was seventeen and stayed away

Belle Glade memorial to the victims of the 1928 flood, which claimed between 1,800 and 3,000 lives and was chronicled in Zora Neale Hurston's Their Eyes Were Watching God.

Sugar refinery

nineteen years in Atlanta and New York. He came back. "Once your feet hit the muck you can't ever leave it," he says.

JANUARY 2000

You can buy skinned rabbits by the big tree on MLK where the men play dominoes and keep warm in the cold by burning scrap wood and trash in a big barrel. When the cane fields are burned and harvested—that's how they do it—great clouds of smoke billow on the horizon, the Belle Glade air flutters with black ash and an acrid tang, and the rabbits living among the tall cane sprint for safety where the luckless among them encounter men and boys, waiting to pounce, who chase and beat them with a piece of cane, a stick, or an occasional five-iron. Run rabbits, and football comes easy. At least this is the nearly official single best explanation for why this town of fifteen thousand produces so much football talent. Like much in a place that appears to exist in the half-light between reality and folktale, the story seems at once fantastic and true.

After high school, Lester Finney left Belle Glade on a football scholarship to McPherson College in Kansas. "I didn't want no part of Belle Glade," he says. But he came back. Finney makes T-shirts—he makes the King Day shirts—in a grim-looking edifice on King with its street-side mural of Tupac Shakur and Biggie Smalls, both shot dead in their twenties in seeming fulfillment of the feuding thug life they rapped about.

Fluently artful, Finney personalizes the designs freehand while his home-made chicken-wire-and-spit dryer creaks and squeaks the freshly silk-screened shirts along. Throughout, he holds forth, evenly, intently, the pitch of his voice rising slightly for emphasis, preaching, teaching, analyzing, inquiring, entertaining, and enjoying the parade of folks who stop by, ostensibly to order a shirt, or pick up one, or check on one, but mostly for a fix of Finney.

Artist, entrepreneur, musician, rapper, motivational speaker, civic leader, inventor, role model, surrogate parent, Finney is the neighborhood paladin, guru,

Robert Hardnett, running rabbits. When the cane fields burn, the rabbits run.

Robert Hardnett, cane catch. The rabbits sell for two dollars a head, sometimes for more to out-of-towners.

herald, and pal, his cluttered shop a sanctuary, safe and warm. He is also, as Muhammad Lester Finney, the Nation of Islam's man in the muck, donning a gray suit and bow tie to sell *The Final Call* on King.

"I don't care who knows that I helped somebody," he says. "I'm just here to see the results."

Across King, next to Betty's Beauty Salon, is the Sudsy City Laundromat, the domain of Annie Williams, its estimable manager, who lives next door with her two foster boys—"I'm their mamma and daddy," she says. The laundry is owned by the Houstons, Belle Glade's old-moneyed black family. They also own the Dunkin' Donuts on the highway, where Williams makes the doughnuts each morning. Williams has the hard stare of a hard life and the exuberant laugh of someone who has enjoyed it nonetheless. At forty she has been sober and clean of crack and drink for thirteen years, February 3, a particular accomplishment on a street where both are amply evident day in, day out. "It's hard," she says. "It's really hard. You really have to burn to live."

Williams trains her stare on a crack addict skulking by a boarded-up building across King. She has made it her business to keep that abandoned building empty until it can be razed. James Leonard, the hairstylist, her best friend, laments the city's failure to fix up the street. "They've tried, I done been in the meetings," says Williams. "The people got to improve, James. The people got to improve."

Little on King escapes Williams's attention. "You missed it," she tells us later, "it" being a flatbed truck of strippers that had stopped in the patchy parking lot at Tiny's liquor store—a squat oasis of gleaming pints two blocks up King. They were advertising a Miami club, in the flesh.

Tiny's proprietor is W. T. "Gus" Miles. Gruff around the edges, Miles talks about what he has lost—of his friends growing up "ain't but four of us left alive"—and what he has found. "My goal is to become a good Muslim." The Million Man March changed his life. "You see black men hugging each other, crying, you never seen no love like that. I did cocaine, I did all that, but I never had nothing felt that good."

Desolate in the brightest light, King Boulevard comes alive with the dimming of day.

Tiny's pints make their move. The sweet thick smoke of Collins barbecue perfumes the night air, seducing with every breath. On the street in front of Finney's, young men gather. Roy Smith—Saint King Roy his apparent show business name—approaches, launching into a dazzling, frenzied song and dance, hoping to earn some money for a rock of crack. "Ya'll ever heard of Carbona spot remover?" he asks brightly, describing an apocalyptic vision—Jesus, chariots, and all—he experienced after sniffing some.

"If you help black people you're going to help everybody," says Finney,

Muhammad Lester Finney—artist, entrepreneur, inventor, mentor, and minister of the Nation of Islam

working into the Saturday night. "Black people is a burden on people. The Bible refer to man as he made from dust. When you look at the way black people hang around the streets, they hang out just like dust hang on your furniture. And they even got a term where they call it the street sweep, which means get rid of the brothers hanging on the corner."

Who uses that expression? "The police," says Finney, accent on the first syllable.

We attend Sunday services at Leviticus Temple of Praise, Church of God in Christ, a storefront church on King. We stopped by earlier in the week to meet the pastor. "Pastor dead," said a small child playing out front. Inside, Evangelist

Annie Williams

Evelyn Little, preparing the church for the first services since her son, the pastor, Johnny Frank Hines, Jr., died twelve days ago at thirty-four, tells us our visit is a sign and comfort. Sunday's service is anguished and euphoric. It ends with the parishioners spilling into the parking lot, holding hands in a circle, singing "We Shall Overcome" on King.

Across from Leviticus is a Haitian church, and walking along King on Sunday afternoon we are lured to the lilting tambourine joy of a Jamaican Seventh-day Adventist revival going on in the loading ramp where migrant workers assemble each morning before dawn. The African diaspora reconvenes in Belle Glade—African Americans, Jamaicans, and Haitians, African peoples sundered by slavery all drawn back together by the muck.

A few white officials participate in the Martin Luther King Day Parade, but the after-parade program at St. Paul Church of God in Christ and the dinner that follows at St. John First Missionary Baptist Church are basically all-black

"Saint King" Roy Smith

affairs. "I think there's some kind of physical fear," says Harma Miller at St. John. What white people don't realize, she says, is "we're just as scared as they are when we go among their people."

Miller picked vegetables until she was twelve, the youngest of six daughters of a migrant crew chief. Despite a predilection to show up at St. John in outfits so loud they could wake the dead, Miller is nobody's fool.

She is, in fact, the mayor of Belle Glade, and like many first families in the black community, with her husband, Henry, she owns and runs a funeral home—Miller Mortuary at Third and MLK. She teaches adults English as a second language at Lakeshore Middle School at Tenth and MLK. She is small, sharp, sure.

"I'm a funeral director. I have a floral design license. I teach and train teach-

Asha Collier, St. John First Missionary Baptist Church

Freddy the Gator, South Florida Water Management mascot, Martin Luther King Day Parade

ers and I speak all of the Romance languages. All six of us girls went to college and all of us have more than one job. Four of us do real estate on the side. I made more money on my eight houses than I do teaching."

Her children, Harva and Heath, are both graduates of Howard University in Washington. Harma produced Harva's rhythm and blues CD. And Heath, Harma's confidant and alter ego, has been managing her campaigns since he was a teenager.

The mayor is picked from among the commissioners, and while Miller has served as mayor before, this past few months has been the first time the commission has had a black majority, and that has made all the difference. It was a long time coming. Even though whites are only 14 percent of Belle Glade's fifteen thousand people, the city held its local elections not in March, like all its neighbors, but in September, when many migrant workers are away. The new black majority voted to move Election Day to March, effective 2002. They voted to hire the first black city manager.

It was Henry Miller who, with other local members of Martin Luther King's fraternity, Alpha Phi Alpha, petitioned to have a street named for King. Harma Miller was on the commission that approved it.

Not long after returning home from Belle Glade, we received a phone call from the Reverend J. Richard Harris, an assistant pastor at St. John, saying that he had heard about our visit and that we had missed him.

Harris has a remarkable talent, a gift, for which there is no precise word in the English language. Through a combination of charisma, chutzpah, cunning, and cool, he has a knack for being where it's at and looking as if that is right where he belongs.

For example: Harris, who has fashioned his Mountain Movers Ministry to

Wilbert Sime, Haitian migrant worker

attend to the spiritual needs of professional football players (he is planning on writing a book, "Pampered and Pimped: The Black Athlete in America"), attended Super Bowl XXXIV in January 2000 at the Georgia Dome (just off MLK Drive) in Atlanta. The St. Louis Rams defeated the Tennessee Titans, and after the game, Harris stopped by the Titans' locker room. "I always go to the losers' locker room first," he explains. After Harris offered words of comfort to the team, the Titans coach Jeff Fisher thanked him, and they walked out before the waiting cameras together. Folks back home in Belle Glade watching the game on TV were shocked to see Harris side by side with Fisher. Even while it was happening, Harris got calls on his cell phone from back home. "When you become coach with the Titans, Rev?"

The next day Harris learned that the Baltimore Ravens star linebacker Ray

Mayor Harma Miller

The Reverend J. Richard Harris

Lewis and two associates had been charged with the murder of two men in a brawl after a Super Bowl party in Atlanta. Lewis is from Lakeland, Florida, and Harris, who knew him from high school football there, quickly managed a jailhouse visit. "You know why you're here?" Harris asked Lewis. "God is trying to get your attention." He emerged as Lewis's spiritual counselor. Every day at the Lewis trial—held at the Fulton County Courthouse on MLK in Atlanta—there was Harris, sitting right behind the defendant. He organized a prayer vigil. The case against Lewis collapsed. He pleaded guilty to obstruction of justice and was given a suspended sentence. His two codefendants were found innocent.

NOVEMBER 2000

We return to Belle Glade for the annual Muck Bowl football classic pitting Glades Central against neighboring Pahokee, but because it falls on the Friday after the 2000 election, we find ourselves thick in the muck of the disputed

Florida vote in the presidential election. Belle Glade is in Palm Beach County, the eye of the storm.

At a single polling place on MLK in Belle Glade, Gore received 768 votes and Bush 9, but another 157 voted for more than one candidate on the now famously confusing butterfly ballot, and another 40 had not successfully punched clean any chad. Same story, if somewhat less dramatic, at the other polling place on King.

Two months earlier, on September 12, Harma Miller and another black candidate, Mary Ross Wilkerson, had won more votes than they had in the past for city commission but lost to two white candidates in a landslide. The ballot box, Miller charged, had been stuffed. Belle Glade's first-ever black majority was gone.

The Muck Bowl results are beyond dispute. The Glades Central Raiders, on

Glades Central High School water boy Thomas Lawrence at the Muck Bowl

their way to a third straight state title and in the midst of what will be a forty-seven-game winning streak, defeat Pahokee, 41 to 7.

On the sidelines, helping out, are two friends, twins of modesty and grace, Roosevelt Blackmon and JaJuan Seider. In the storied annals of Glades football, each has had his storybook moments.

Blackmon's story was so unlikely it was the subject of an NFL film, *Two Roads to Glory*, comparing the very different paths to the pros of the golden boy quarterback Peyton Manning and the out-of-the-muck cornerback Blackmon, who even before he was born was known as Tadpole because his father went by the nickname Frog. "His is the story of a road never traveled, a path from obscurity to the brink of a career with the NFL's most storied franchise," the narrator intones.

Blackmon played only a year of high school ball, then after digging graves and selling cars for a while, headed to Morris Brown College on MLK in Atlanta, only to find on his arrival that he was not properly enrolled. Too embarrassed to return home, he stayed, worked nights stocking shelves at the Winn-Dixie on King and days as the Morris Brown football team's water boy and equipment manager. Eventually he became a Morris Brown student and football star, most memorably returning back-to-back eighty-eight-yard punt returns for touchdowns in a 1996 game against Alabama A&M.

In 1998 Peyton Manning was the NFL's number-one draft choice, going to the Indianapolis Colts; Blackmon was a fourth-round draft pick of the Green Bay Packers. He played three games for Green Bay, and seventeen for the Cincinnati Bengals in 1998 and 1999 before an injury ended his NFL career.

In 1992 Seider, a quarterback, caught a halfback option pass to score the winning touchdown in Belle Glade's 21–20 Muck Bowl victory. In 1999, after three years on the bench at West Virginia University, he transferred his senior year to Florida A. & M. Filling in for the starting quarterback, he passed for a near-school-record 238 yards, won the job, led the team into its division semifinals, and was named black college offensive player of the year. In April 2000, the San Diego Chargers made him a sixth-round draft choice.

In August the Chargers released him. The week before, his brother, Jyron Seider, a seventeen-year-old defensive tackle for the Raiders, was shot to death while watching a dice game in an empty lot next to Finney's on King. He was just killing time until his girlfriend, who was having her hair braided, was ready to be picked up. Shortly after midnight the call came to the Seiders' home. "I just fell on my knees," his mother, Cathy, recalls. "I told that boy that those corners going to still be here when he's dead and gone."

Cathy Seider loves Belle Glade. "My mama raised ten kids here. The oldest one is in Atlanta. I think he's moving back here. I wouldn't trade Belle Glade for nothing."

Nearly two thousand people came to her son's funeral (Miller Mortuary buried him), which was held at the high school. "They came from all sides of the tracks, which is what people call it here," says his father, Jay, the athletic director at Glades Central, who is white and who moved to Belle Glade from Buffalo, New York. The Raiders dedicated their 2000 season to Jyron Seider. There is a moment of silence at the Muck Bowl.

Finney, as usual, made the Muck Bowl T-shirts, as well this year as a "Go Glades Central" car-top neon sign that plugs into the car's cigarette lighter. He also made the memorial T-shirts for Jyron Seider, another page, as it were, in Lester Finney's polyester-and-cotton annals of the life and times of Belle Glade.

The day after the Muck Bowl some women stop by to order more memorial T-shirts for a friend who drowned in the canal when she ran off the road driving to West Palm Beach. Her boyfriend escaped, but she was trapped in her seat belt, though an air bubble enabled her to use her cell phone. "It was there long enough for her to call 911 and instruct them on where she was, and then she drowned," Finney explains.

Some other young women drop by, one with an infant. Finney puts on a cut from his self-produced rap CD, *Message to the People*, and raps along with himself. "Hey you, pretty little girl, you slow down now, you're growing up too fast. Like to get attention in the way that you can, even if it's the attention of a full-grown man. Hey you, pretty little girl. Let's slow it down now. Don't grow up too fast." A couple of the girls join in harmony.

Walter Brown, a friend since childhood, stops by to check on some youth football uniforms. When they start reminiscing about their mothers, Finney croons his paean to mother love. Brown recalls that when he was in trouble his mother would cry out, "Dailasha!" He doesn't know the spelling and never heard anyone but his mother say it, but everyone in his family took its meaning. "Get your head down and toot your ass up, it belongs to me."

Brenda Burney drives up. She grew up with Finney, moved away when she was twelve, but still stops by from West Palm Beach every other Saturday. In 1990 she survived being shot six times by a jealous boyfriend—four .38s and two .45s. "I've got a .45 in my leg now," she declares. Burney was one of eight girls and a boy growing up. Finney did all the girls' hair. "My mama don't play," says Burney. "This is the only guy she trusted with his hand in our hairs. I'm telling you this guy can do anything. This guy could have been a cosmetologist."

The Monday after the Muck Bowl there is a march and rally in West Palm

Lakeshia Sanders and Roshell Williams with daughter Court'Tacious Foster at Lester Finney's T-shirt shop

6th Street and Martin Luther King

led by the Reverend Jesse Jackson demanding a recount or revote. On the ride over, Heath Miller, now the assistant band director at the high school and chorus director at Lake Shore Middle, describes his disillusionment since returning to Belle Glade. "At Howard, I learned how to be politically active without being militant, and I despise people who are militant. I think you can go too far and be too angry, and I try to stay away from that." But, he says, the ugliness of the campaign against his mother changed him. "I'm really trying hard not to hate white people. It's sad that it's gotten to the point that I really feel that way."

In the six days since the presidential election, the Reverend J. Richard Harris has emerged as a prominent figure in the postelection protests, even though he couldn't vote. He is a convicted felon, having served less than a year back in the mid-1970s for cashing a few hundred dollars in traveler's checks he had reported stolen in the midst of what this prodigal son of the Glades recounts as a long sojourn in the shady vineyards of music promotion. His most recent arrest, in October, came at a Tampa Bay Buccaneers game at their stadium on Tampa's MLK. Reporters are allowed on the sidelines the last few minutes of the game, and while Harris had press credentials from an Atlanta weekly he sometimes writes for, the police saw it differently.

Harris's first arrest came when he was a teenager in Belle Glade and tried to buy ice cream from the "white" window at the Polar Bear stand. In college at Florida A. & M., when Martin Luther King was assassinated, Harris was part of an armed student uprising that shut down the school. And that summer, back in Belle Glade, he says he and some friends scored some dynamite with an eye to blowing up Tiny's liquors and some other then-white-owned businesses on the black side of town. They could never find a time to blow up Tiny's when some black person might not be hurt, so instead settled for some late-night firebombings, for which they were never caught.

On their separate arrivals in West Palm Beach, Harris and Heath Miller hook up with fluid efficiency. Within moments they are leading the march. At the first contentious rally at the plaza outside the county election headquarters, Harris precedes Jesse Jackson to the microphone, and at the larger subsequent rally at a nearby amphitheater it is Harris who carefully sets up Jackson's lectern.

"There is a direct line from Selma to Florida," Jackson declares, linking the 2000 election dispute to the voting rights struggles of thirty-five years previous. Heath, in the very front of the sea of exultant protesters, beams, nodding as his parents, who have been waiting in the wings, are pulled onstage.

We leave, but from time to time, the muck calls and we call the muck.

In November 2001, Finney reports Glades Central defeated Pahokee again in the Muck Bowl, and his Muck Bowl T-shirts this year carried the legend "Collard Greens, Wild Rabbit, Fried Gator. That's What It Takes to Be a Raider." Earlier, over the summer, two guys from the corner shot and killed each other. "They were both my kids," says Finney. He made memorial T-shirts. And Belle Glade was all over the news just after September 11 when it was reported that Mohamed Atta, believed to have piloted one of the jets into the World Trade Center, had been in the city at least twice in the months before the attack. He came to inquire about crop dusters.

In March 2002, blacks recaptured their majority on the city commission when two black candidates overwhelmingly defeated two white incumbents. The victors were Mary Kendall and—and this is how his name appeared on the ballot—Albert "Secret Squirrel" Dowdell III, who earned his nickname while working as an undercover cop in Belle Glade, as he put it, "like Baretta."

As for the Reverend J. Richard Harris, we have talked to him many times since, but one could also track his progress in the headlines. In April, credentialed by the International Human Rights Association of American Minorities, Harris spoke at the fifty-eighth session of the United Nations Commission on Human Rights in Geneva.

On June 21, 2002, according to a story in *The Palm Beach Post*, Harris walked into the county elections office, produced a certificate from the Board of Executive Clemency showing that his civil rights had been restored, and said he wanted to both register to vote and file as a candidate for the Palm Beach County Commission. The paper quoted Supervisor of Elections Theresa LePore—she who designed the butterfly ballot—as saying, "It's a free country. It's not my place to judge."

Harris, who became the Democratic nominee but was defeated in the general election, says he decided to challenge the incumbent, Tony Masilotti, when Masilotti arranged to name a community gymnasium on MLK in Belle Glade after a white longtime member of the city and county commission.

And, in the Sunday *New York Times*, July 21, 2002, on page 14 there is a big story under the headline "War Chest Is Lacking, but Dance Card Is Full." It recounts former Attorney General Janet Reno's efforts to raise money for her gubernatorial campaign, in this case holding a Janet Reno Dance Party at Level, one of the hottest clubs in Miami's South Beach. A large accompanying photo shows Reno in the midst of a mob, dancing delightedly with an unidentified black man. They are both smiling, looking directly into each other's eyes, their hands raised in twin poses of revelry. Reno's dance partner is, well, of course, the Reverend J. Richard Harris of Belle Glade, Florida.

Afternoon light, Martin Luther King Boulevard

Chapter 3

The Mecca

"We start it. We end it. MBC."

Morris Brown College chant

Martin Luther King Jr. Drive in Atlanta is a big, important street, be-
fitting the honor due King in his hometown. Ten miles long, it takes you the
places most King streets do, and it takes you places most King streets don't.

The Busy Bee Café—a snug shrine to chitlins, chicken gizzards, and neck
bones "slow-cooked to bone-sucking perfection"—is on King. Booker T. Washington High School, King's own alma mater, is on King. (As is, with perfect symmetry, the Booker T. Washington High School in Tuskegee, Alabama, where
King's antecedent as America's most publicly honored African American most
famously lived and is buried.)

But King Drive also threads its way through the sinews of downtown Atlanta, past the state capitol, the World of Coca-Cola, Underground Atlanta, the
Fulton County Courthouse—where Jamil Abdullah Al-Amin, née H. Rap
Brown, the iconic black radical cum Muslim cleric, was convicted of murder,
and Ray Lewis, the iconic black athlete, was not—and, most evocatively, the
twin towers of the James H. "Sloppy" Floyd Building. Located at what is now

Saturday night at Martin Luther King Drive and Sunset, Atlanta

Confederate graves in Oakland Cemetery, where Atlanta's Martin Luther King Drive dead-ends

2 Martin Luther King Drive, the towers are named for the powerful white law-maker who in 1965 led the ultimately unsuccessful effort to keep Julian Bond from being seated in the Georgia House of Representatives after he was duly elected, because of his opposition to the Vietnam War and the draft. On January 14, 1966, King led a march on Bond's behalf down what is now King to the capitol.

Before it is through, King Drive makes one last daring foray across the city's symbolic landscape, advancing east from downtown to Oakland Cemetery, dead-ending at the pastoral last resting place of Margaret Mitchell, the author of *Gone with the Wind*, of twenty-four Atlanta mayors, of five Confederate generals, and of nearly three thousand Confederate dead, their acres of simple white-cross rows sanctified by a three-story obelisk and the melancholy witness of the fifteen-ton marble Lion of Atlanta, grand, defeated, spent, but still clenching in his paw a piece of the Confederate flag on which he lays.

For all the places it goes, the center of gravity of Atlanta's MLK can be precisely pinpointed—the intersection of King Drive and Sunset Avenue in the midst of the campus of Morris Brown College.

"It's the original FUBU," said Terry Thomas, a schoolteacher and 1981 Morris Brown alumni who told us about the school after the King Day Parade down the MLK in Belle Glade, Florida. For Us By Us. While the other more well-known and prestigious schools that adjoin Morris Brown and together compose the Atlanta University Center—Morehouse College, Spelman College, and Clark Atlanta University—were founded by whites for blacks, Morris Brown was founded in 1881 by the African Methodist Episcopal Church. It prides itself on taking students as it

Brownite induction ceremony, Freshman Week, Morris Brown College

finds them, a school with an open door and a minuscule endowment. Martin Luther King went to Morehouse, but his mother, Alberta, went to Morris Brown as an adult. Before our visit to Belle Glade, we had never heard of Morris Brown College. In August 2000, we spend Freshman Week there.

The Alma Mater

On a raised circular cement pedestal on the main yard at Morris Brown, Herman "Skip" Mason, the young dean of students, with a shaved head and serious mien, is trying to coax, cow, and command several hundred new freshmen gathered round into learning the school song. It is getting to the end of Freshman Week. It is August, and it is hot, dripping hot.

"Those people who are perpetrating and faking, you had all week to learn two verses of a song," says Mason, a historian, librarian, and minister by training. All week long he has been on the students about learning the song and about wearing their purple-and-white Morris Brown freshman beanies.

Markeevius Smith, eighteen, is tired. Marching band practice went well past midnight, and as a prospective member of the band he was called to campus weeks before Freshman Week to begin rehearsing. Smith plays French horn—"an instrument that requires talent," he says, comparing it with his former instrument, the loud and showy trumpet, "our enemy." Recruited by the army and navy for his horn, Smith played in the band back home in Thomaston, Georgia, marching along the Martin Luther King Drive there to Lincoln Park on Emancipation Day, an occasion that Thomaston has been celebrating every year since 1865. But the Thomaston band marched in the shuffling white style, says Smith, demonstrating. Morris Brown marches in the high-kicking black style. New muscles ache.

Speaking through a megaphone, Mason commands the students to come in tighter together, to link hands. "It's too hot to be with all these black folk," mutters a large young woman as she moseys forward.

"There comes a time, brothers and sisters, when you have to get serious," says Mason. "This is not high school. This is college. Let us sing the alma mater."

The students sway together in song.

"Tomorrow we are inducting you into our family," says Mason, himself a Morris Brown alum. They take this family metaphor seriously. Many students have family, sometimes lots of family, who also went to Morris Brown. Many are members of the founding AME Church.

"It's a love that you take to your grave," says Andre Williams, a self-possessed twenty-two-year-old senior from Lexington, Kentucky, who is vice president of the student government. "Cut you and you bleed purple." Only last year Williams was set to transfer out of Morris Brown because he found their business program wanting. A dean pleaded with him not to leave. He promised that the program would improve. He stayed and it did, Williams says.

These students' languor about the song and their cool toward the beanies notwithstanding, Freshman Week has been one of often frenzied high spirits and what seems a deep and instant camaraderie.

Kedist Hirpassa

"I've never felt so much positive energy in my whole entire life from African Americans," says Kedist Hirpassa. It is late Saturday, and she is by herself in the empty stands at Morris Brown's Herndon Stadium as the football team scrimmages and the cheerleaders thrust and shout in the blazing sunshine. Hirpassa has the dashing passions and headlong confidence of the young and sure. Even as she is contemplating transferring out of Morris Brown after a semester, she is running for freshman class president. Last night she lip-synched backup vocals to "Proud Mary" to help a friend competing in the Miss Freshman Pageant in front of an ecstatic freshman class crammed into the withering warmth of the unair-conditioned auditorium.

Hirpassa's first semester is like that. She is elected class president, but when the runner-up challenges the results, the election is left unresolved. She is Morris Brown's entry in the Miss AUC Freshman contest. She writes for the *AUC Digest*, a campus newspaper. She interns at the governor's office.

But even as she throws herself into the middle of everything, she remains a loner, reserved, observing, the calm in the storm of her own life. She is different. She was born in Ethiopia; her parents came from warring Ethiopian tribes—her father's urban, light-skinned with European features; her mother's rural, dark-skinned, despised by her father's tribe. Her mother brought her to the United States when she was five, and she grew up at a succession of boarding and public schools, finishing high school in Washington's Maryland suburbs.

In her Ethiopian circles, her choice of a black college was not considered smart. She picked Morris Brown after going on a Freedom Ride tour that ended in Atlanta organized by C. DeLores Tucker, head of the National Political Congress of Black Women and a friend of the King family, who when Hirpassa was in seventh grade "took me into her arms," Hirpassa says, and has been a mentor ever since. (Tucker is best known for her campaign against gangsta rap, a campaign in which she enlisted Hirpassa, who nonetheless admits a soft spot for Tucker's nemesis, the late Tupac Shakur.)

Morris Brown freshman Kedist Hirpassa at Big Bethel AME Church

African American by definition, Hirpassa finds her first months on King Drive a twisting trek through the maze of her own relationship to blackness.

"It has helped me realize that I am black," she says. She loves the mix of black people and has come to appreciate black styles that once bewildered her. But, after recalling the times her use of standard English or taste in music has been dismissed as "white," she is back in the maze. Sometimes, she says, "being in an all-black school I don't feel like I'm black. I feel like I have more in common with a white person than a black person." She gets frustrated by the school's inefficiencies, "how things never get done." When she complains, a woman who works at the college wisecracks, "Girl, didn't you know this was a black school?" Hirpassa is not amused.

And from early on, Hirpassa is aware how the students from the other AUC schools "frown down" on Morris Brown as the "ghetto" school. "A lot of More-house guys, especially the ones I've met, they automatically assume I go to Spelman, and when I say, 'No, I go to Morris Brown,' their reaction is, 'You go to Morris Brown?' Like, you know, very disgusted. You know, it's like they have this really bad reputation. They even had in their Morehouse school paper, they said something like, 'My wife goes to Spelman, my girlfriend goes to Clark, and my "ho" goes to Morris Brown.' "

Olive Branch

The Olive Branch ceremonies the last Saturday of Freshman Week are designed to tamp down the interschool rivalries that in the days previous have been whipped to a fine froth. The men all meet at the Morris Brown gym, Skip Mason presiding.

He leads the singing of the Negro National Anthem. "All these schools that are represented here today," says Mason, "were founded in the shadows of slavery."

He is followed by Andre Williams, the Morris Brown senior. "Look around the room," says Williams. "Look at all the different shades of black."

The main address, a stentorian stem-winder, is delivered by Alexander Hamilton VI, who teaches at Morris Brown and is president of the Coalition for Young Black Ministers. "Everybody wants to talk about the American dream. Nobody wants to talk about the American nightmare," he hollers. "There's something wrong in America when a black man has a better chance of having a seat in the electric chair in Texas than he does a chair in a classroom at Texas A&M University.

"Don't be miseducated," Hamilton says, ending his peroration. "I got love for you Negroes! I got love for you Negroes! I got love for you Negroes!"

Outside afterward, two Morehouse juniors—Ashanti Johnson and Don Smith—are underwhelmed by Hamilton's performance, which they consider out of date and over the top. "One thing that brought us here, even if we don't know it, is that for these four years that we're here, we're not in the minority," says Smith, who like Johnson is in a five-year engineering program that connects Morehouse to Georgia Tech. "It's like a parallel life."

Johnson says being at Morehouse helped him survive chemistry. At a majority-white school he might have quit when it got really tough. "I would have blamed it on racism. Here you don't have those crutches to fall back on." Being at Morehouse has made him more self-assured in the everyday of race relating, like when he goes shopping at the upscale Lenox Square Mall in Buckhead. "Before, I would go in and make sure I speak to everybody working in the store so they don't think I'm stealing anything." Now, "I just demand respect."

But even in this black parallel universe, Johnson still finds himself shadow-boxing with race. The son of a corporate executive, Johnson went to high school in Des Moines, Iowa, and Jackson, Mississippi, a football star and honors student. That, and his being black, was too much for some peers to assimilate. He decided not to play football at college, because even at a black school, "I don't want to be seen as that dumb black jock in class when I actually have higher SAT scores, a higher grade point average."

That Morris Brown spirit: Falana Flowers and other Morris Brown students before the Olive Branch ceremony

Herndon Stadium, Morris Brown College

(When we talk a year later, Johnson says he shouldn't have cared so much what people might think. He loves football and should have played. Moreover, "I look at why I chose chemistry. I wanted to go against the norm." He is switching to international relations.)

After the separate men's and women's Olive Branch ceremonies, the students march, thousands in all, to a party in the Clark Atlanta Stadium on King, chanting their loyalties along the way: "Ashes to ashes, dust to dust. You got to be a Morehouse man to party like us." The Morris Brown reply is simple, direct: "We start it. We end it. MBC."

There is so much talk about Atlanta being a black mecca, but to be part of this dazzling parade of black youth, together for the first time, stretching as far as the eye can see, must be a nearly religious experience, though the soundtrack at the stadium is more Mystikal than mystical: "Shake ya ass. But watch ya self. Shake ya ass. Show me what you're working with."

Alex Jones, Stephenson High School Band, Herndon Stadium

Diagonally across King, twenty thousand fans, a family crowd, fill Herndon Stadium for a high school football doubleheader. The four-hundred-strong band from Southwest DeKalb High School is wailing brass, thundering drums. In the distance, the Atlanta skyline is set off against heavens of charcoal, blue, and black. The intersection of King and Sunset is ablaze in light and motion and the intermingling sounds of rap and football, cruising and greeting, of Saturday night in a safe, happy, entirely black, and very beautiful world. The mule-drawn caisson carrying King's body rolled past here. Less than half a mile up Sunset is the modest home that King, amid his travails in Selma, Alabama, bought in 1965 for ten thousand dollars. Coretta Scott King still lives there, within distant earshot of the revelry.

Shedding the Beanies

Sunday evening is the Brownite induction ceremony. Because there is such a large freshman class, it is held in the gym instead of the chapel, and in the confusion, there is no sound system. In a very Morris Brown, make-do moment, everybody must address the hallowed gathering using Skip Mason's megaphone.

Football spectators, Herndon Stadium

"I know many of you had other choices and you could have gone other places but I also know that for some of you this was the only choice and for some of you this was the only place that would take you in with the academic shortcoming you had but yet and still, they had the courage to look beyond all your faults and they saw your needs," says Mason.

As they sing "Give Me That Old Morris Brown Spirit," to the tune of "Give Me That Old Time Religion," the 963 members of the class of 2004 file across the gym floor, one by one shedding their beanies and approaching Dolores Cross, who came to Morris Brown from the presidency of Chicago State, also on King Drive, in the fall of 1998.

Cross is a marathon runner. She is direct and modest, elegant with a shy smile. She never lived in the South, never attended a historically black college, and is not a member of the AME Church. She is an outsider. As the students approach Cross, many shake hands, but many also throw themselves into her in full, reciprocated embrace. It is as if they are graduating from college, not just setting out. They are graduating to Morris Brown.

"Will you succeed?" Cross asks the throng when the last beanie is cast aside, the last hug had. "Yes!" they shout back in reply.

"Will you give something back?" "Yes!"

"Will you stay in touch?" "Yes!"

Before leaving Atlanta, we visit Morehouse College to meet a couple of young men from Belle Glade who are students there. The administrator who recruited them and others from the Glades whom he is excited for us to meet says we all need to stop by the school's public relations office first. There, the two women in charge greet us with suspicion. We are interrogated about our purpose. Our account of our journey along King is met with doubt and disdain. They are especially keen on establishing that Morehouse is not connected to Morris Brown. We are given a pass that permits us to remain at a single spot on campus— outside King chapel—for one hour.

Our spirits are revived at Best Buy Casket and Urns, nestled in a dreary strip mall just across King Drive from Westview Cemetery, whose well-known inhabitants include Joel Chandler Harris, the white man who collected and popular-

William Bacon at Best Buy Caskets

ized the Uncle Remus stories. From the cheery painting of a tropical sunset on its plate-glass front window, Best Buy looks like an inexpensive West Indian restaurant. Perhaps it is a vision of the paradise awaiting someone laid to rest in a solid Breckenridge cherry casket with velvet crepe interior, adjustable bed, and memory tube, a $4,995 value for only $2,195. Inside, the salesman, William Bacon, smiles with bright delight as we talk about our mission. "I love what you guys are doing." He says he wishes he could go along.

Morris Brown Redux

When we see Kedist Hirpassa during winter break back in Washington, she is working in C. DeLores Tucker's office, helping to provide the Bush administration with the names of black women qualified for top federal appointments. When we visit Atlanta in the spring, she is the youngest and only black member of a socialist group that meets at Georgia State. She has written a play based on a dream she had about a biracial girl in 1940s Mississippi with ambitions to be a great actress, which she hopes to get produced by an AUC theater group.

In the fall of 2001, she transfers to Georgia State University, but even as she moves to a majority-white school, she starts a new organization with a few students from the various AUC campuses. It is called African Brothers and Sisters. They plan to create a magazine, to read to kids in the projects along King, to agitate for reparations.

In the spring of 2002, Dr. Cross leaves the presidency of Morris Brown. By late fall, creditors and accreditors are after Morris Brown, and by 2003 the college is in the not unfamiliar position of being on the verge of going out of business.

Chapter 4

The Buckle on the Black Belt

Wait until you see a congregation of more than two dark-complected people. If they can't agree on a single solitary thing, then you can go off satisfied. Those are My People.

Zora Neale Hurston, "My People, My People!"
from Dust Tracks on a Road, *1937*

At seventy-three, Marion Tumbleweed Beach is small and, in her braids and little African hat, at once captivating and ferocious. Few people have lived lives so sinuously intertwined, so passionately engaged, with the black American journey across the twentieth century—as a teacher, writer, poet, reporter, and editor, as an activist and an intellectual. Her roaring, riveting recounting of her life comes fast and furious, with lyrical, spiky abandon. She is Miss Jane Pittman on speed.

It is September 2000, days before Selma, Alabama's climactic mayoral run-off election in which a black candidate, James Perkins, Jr., in his third go at it, looks to be on the verge of finally defeating the white incumbent, Joseph T. Smitherman. Volunteers, white and black, young and old—even Martin Luther King III—are streaming in from across the country to help Perkins make history. A legion of journalists is amassing to bear witness. Once again, the eyes

Chasity Shears, First Baptist Church, Selma, Alabama

Martin Luther King III talking with college students at September 2000 Get Out the Vote rally, Ronnie Sharp Park

of a nation will cast their gaze—however fleetingly this time—on little Selma, bloody Selma, to see if the narrative of the black voting-rights struggle that stirred the nation's soul thirty-five years before will reach its ordained if belated conclusion here in the cradle of that crusade. Amid this familiar tableau, it is not hard to pick out which house on Selma's Martin Luther King Street belongs to Marion Tumbleweed Beach.

It's the only house with a fairy-tale garden, front and back, lush with honeysuckle and holly, camellias, crepe myrtle, pussy willows, English ivy, and maidenhair ferns; azaleas, dogwoods (white and red), tulip trees, palms and peaches, figs, blueberries, blackberries, lemons, limes and satsuma oranges; three varieties of bananas, peanuts, pecans, peppers, tomatoes, collard greens; and nestled within their collective embrace, homemade shrines to a few favorite Catholic saints. It's the only house flying a red, black, and green African liberation flag. And it's the only house with a red-and-white Smitherman sign planted in the front lawn, advertising her support for the man who has been mayor of Selma with only the briefest, self-imposed interruption since Martin Luther King himself marched along what is now Martin Luther King Street.

To say that Tumbleweed—it's the name that suits her and sticks—is at odd ends with sentiment in Selma's black community on this matter is an understatement. "I've caught more hell from blacks than I have from whites," she says. "I've lived with blacks. They had a chance to kick my ass." This woman has more feuds than most people have friends. "I always get tangled up with people. I gain energy when people mess with me."

The talk of Martin Luther King streets from one coast to the other inevitably turns to what it means to be black in America. Marion Tumbleweed Beach is living proof of just how tight the black community is, and how encompassing. If that sounds like a contradiction, it is not. As surely as there is an

Watering her garden, working the phones. At home on Martin Luther King Street in Selma with Marion Tumbleweed Beach.

America, there is a black America. Like America, black America is endlessly, kaleidoscopically diverse.

Want to hear what is right with black folk? Head on down to Martin Luther King. Want to hear what is wrong with black folk? Head directly to Martin Luther King. The notion of some sort of groupthink, of a community speaking with a single voice, is an invention of convenience. It comes from a broader nation and media that want to know what this separate piece of America is thinking and feeling and works backward from certain evidence to provide a logical quote box of explanation.

What unites the black nation along King is a shared terrain, a sense of place and predicament. After that, anything goes. About the only thing that all black folk in America have in common is contending with being black in America, figuring out what it means to be black in America. That turns out to be enough. That turns out to be plenty.

Tumbleweed, who defies the sense of the black community intuited from afar, who cannot be explained off King, makes sense, perfect and absurd, on King.

When we first meet Tumbleweed she is storming toward the National Voting Rights Museum, a citadel of civil rights history and gathering spot for out-of-town folks coming to Selma to lend a hand to the campaign to defeat Smitherman. She is just coming up the street from the Edmund Pettus Bridge, one of the most sacred sites of the civil rights movement, where two white women from New York are standing sentry holding signs informing passing motorists that "Joe Gotta Go." Tumbleweed disagrees.

"Yankee go home!" she screams. "Yankee go home!"

"You're outside agitators," she sneers. "You going to go back home and brag about how you freed us?"

It is a moment of brilliant, bollixing street theater—mad, wise, and ironic—by a woman who cannot countenance the thought that either she or her people would ever take refuge in victimhood. Thirty-five years earlier, in 1965, King

First Baptist Church, Martin Luther King Street, Selma

Iowan Lexi Kiel-Wornson, campaign volunteer

asked Tumbleweed (she had helped with the Montgomery bus boycott and would be with him on the Memphis-to-Jackson Meredith March in 1966 and his campaign in Chicago, where she lived most of her adult life) to come back to Selma to register the "outside agitators" then swarming into town to support the voting rights protests, and to find places for them to stay. Before she arrived, that chore was entirely in the hands of some white New England matrons. "It didn't look good," says Tumbleweed. "It looked like we were still being freed by white abolitionists."

In retrospect, the Selma campaign was, even more than the March on Washington, King's crowning triumph. "There never was a moment in American history more honorable and more inspiring than the pilgrimage of clergymen and laymen of every race and faith pouring into Selma to face danger at the side of the embattled Negroes," said King after leading marchers across the Edmund Pettus Bridge, where (in his absence) they had been beaten on Bloody

Sunday a couple of weeks earlier, and on to Montgomery. "Confrontation of good and evil compressed in the tiny community of Selma generated the massive power to turn the whole nation to a new course."

Compressed is right. Selma still seems in many ways a sleepy small Southern town where they keep time by the train whistle. But the carbon of black-white conflict here has been compressed so long and so hard that Selma is now a gleaming hard diamond of racial antagonism.

A city of twenty thousand, Selma is 70 percent black. It is located in the heart of Alabama's Black Belt, so named for the color of the rich dark earth from which grew the plantations whose legacy to this day is to make the Black Belt the blackest stretch of America. From slavery on, says J. L. Chestnut, the first black lawyer of the twentieth century in Selma (his office is on Jeff Davis, not far from the intersection with MLK) and chairman of the deacon board at First Baptist on King, the overwhelming blackness of the Black Belt produced an especially severe and sanctimonious strain of white supremacy. "I've been here all of my life. I can't think of one damn thing that these people voluntarily did that was positive in terms of healthy race relations between black and white people as equals. I can't name one thing and I am almost seventy years old."

They are always commemorating the battles fought here, whether it's at the Edmund Pettus Bridge or the Battle of Selma, at which General Nathan Bedford Forrest was routed and Selma, the arsenal of the Confederacy, fell, presaging the rebellion's end. To the civil rights movement, Selma was and is sacred space, a place of pilgrimage—to the bridge, to the Voting Rights Museum, and to a two-block stretch of King Street, from Selma Avenue to Jeff Davis Avenue, anchored by two churches, First Baptist and Brown Chapel AME, both built, brick by brick, by newly freed blacks in the early years after emancipation, both home to the movement.

"It's their mecca," says Smitherman.

"One More River to Cross," reads a Perkins campaign flyer under a photo of the Edmund Pettus Bridge. It promises "reconciliation, not revenge."

"Why Change?" asks a full-page Smitherman ad bearing the photos of the blacks who hold nine of the thirteen highest paid positions in Smither-

Moonrise over mural by Edmund Pettus Bridge

man's administration—from police chief to cemetery sexton.

When Smitherman was first elected mayor in 1964, he was the insurgent. Against subsequent white opponents he carried the black vote, and till now, even against black opponents, he got enough black votes to win. In Chestnut's view, Smitherman's first serious black opponent, F. D. Reese (Perkins managed his campaign), made the mistake of soft-pedaling race in vain hopes of getting some white votes but succeeded only in depressing black turnout.

This year Chestnut and his law partners, Hank and Rose Sanders, both Harvard-educated lawyers, made sure that mistake would not be repeated. Hank Sanders is a state senator, and he and Rose are important players in black politics at the local, state, and national levels. In the years to come we encounter Rose and her daughter, Malika, an activist in her own right, at the Million Family March in Washington, where they run the family stage, at the Congressional Black Caucus annual meeting in D.C., and at the State of the Black World Conference in Atlanta. Small, restless, with a voice forever hoarse and a myopic squint, Rose is the founder of the Voting Rights Museum and the guiding force behind the "Joe Gotta Go" campaign. Say "Rose" to a white person in Selma and stand back. She is despised. Far more than Perkins, Smitherman is running against her. "I don't want Rose Sanders taking over the town," he says.

Equally small in stature and intense in temperament, Tumbleweed and Rose do not often see eye to eye. They have gone many rounds over the years. Rose ends each encounter, "I love you, Miss Tumbleweed."

"Patronizing," Tumbleweed sniffs.

Smitherman grew up on the wrong side of the tracks, raised by an aunt who was the head waitress at the Splendid Café, where Tumbleweed's mother was the chef. "You noticed he talks black," says Tumbleweed. "He doesn't talk like a white man." In recent years, Smitherman, a chain smoker, a bit overweight, has

J. L. Chestnut, attorney and elder, First Baptist Church

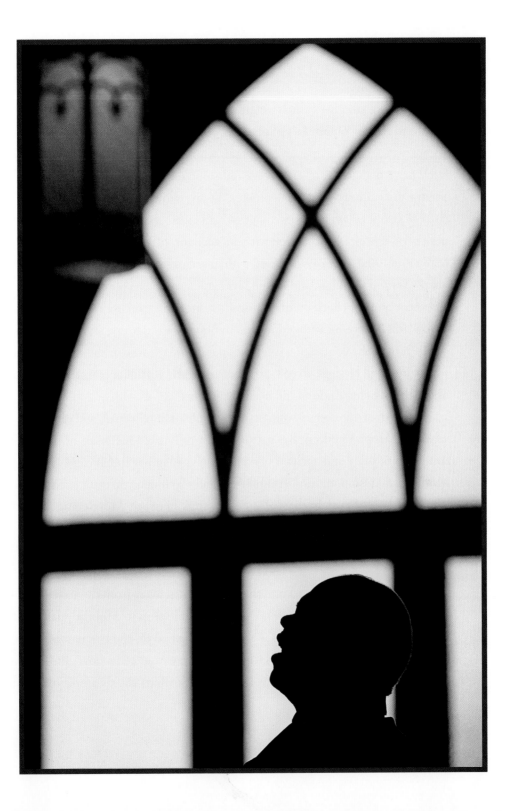

taken his daily constitutional past Tumbleweed's house. She would be sitting in her chair under her sun umbrella, and he would stop. They would talk. It became his routine.

When we stop by Tumbleweed's house hours after our first meeting, she is out front, talking on her cell phone and watering her garden. She offers us seats on her patio, and she asks a young man who seems to appear from nowhere to fetch her wooden box of cigarettes and some daiquiris. It is midafternoon. We assume the daiquiris are nonalcoholic. We are wrong.

For the next two hours, we have our first immersion in the Tumbleweed experience—a tour de force eyewitness account of African American history, orally footnoted and cross-indexed with, it seems, every current of thought since people started thinking, and all too vivid and fantastic to possibly be true, except we discover as we check on one thing after another in the months and years that follow, it is. Our education continues in phone calls, letters, and in the summer of 2002, over the course of a week we spend at her house in the ridiculous hope of getting it all straight. Her stories are endlessly intriguing. And without end. She is the Scheherazade of the black experience.

"She's an extraordinary woman, really brilliant, intellectual, and very learned," says John Hope Franklin, the nation's most renowned historian of the African American odyssey and a friend from their days together in Chicago. But Franklin allows that, sometimes, "Tumbleweed talks so much you can't get a word in."

Tumbleweed was born in Tunnel Springs between Mobile and Selma on March 27, 1927, the 113th anniversary of the Alabama massacre of her great-grandmother's people, the Creek Indians, by forces led by Andrew Jackson. Her great-grandfather was a free black man from Mali who had been told by his father that his destiny lay beyond the African stars, away from the slavers and the French. He made his way by salt caravan and silk ship to Mobile, Alabama, arriving just after the end of the Civil War. On her birth, she was named General Marion Tumbleweed Delores Marie Lett. "They expected a boy," she says, and wanted to name him for the Revolutionary War hero the Swamp Fox, Francis

Tumbleweed

Marion. The doctor knew enough not to record General, but the rest stuck. "I was a preemie, sickle-cell, the whole bit, I was supposed to die," she says. But her great-grandmother the Creek Indian Rilla said, "No, she's a tumbleweed."

Tumbleweed has written the first two volumes of her family saga, "Beyond the African Stars" and "A Red Camellia for Papa," which ends in 1939. She is writing a narrative poem about Mel Fisher, the treasure hunter who salvaged the wreck of the slave ship *Henrietta Marie* in the Florida Straits, and she has spent time at the Mel Fisher museum in Key West researching it. She has a collection of poetry, *Come Ride with Me*, published in Chicago in 1970 (and reissued by Rose and the Voting Rights Museum, though Tumbleweed complains that in some copies pages were stapled together upside down and out of order). On the cover is an illustration of a prickly tumbleweed, and below it the refrain from the song: "Lonely, but free I'll be found, drifting along with the tumbling tumble-weeds."

In Selma, a city exquisitely latticed into compartments of class, family, and color, Tumbleweed goes everywhere, engaging and enraging every which way.

"Booker T. loves you, working with your hands," she sings out, blowing kisses to some Selma sanitation workers in bright orange jumpsuits cleaning up King. One of the men flexes a hand in acknowledgment.

That day we venture off to Tuskegee, where Tumbleweed once studied and her father lived, to pay homage to Booker T. Washington.

From there, we arrive late in the day at the national park at Horseshoe Bend (she calls it by the Creek name, Tohopeka), where Andrew Jackson defeated the Creek Confederacy. The park is quiet. The slender, young white park ranger inside the visitor center is tidying up toward closing. Tumbleweed is not pleased. "What do you do all day?" she asks. "Masturbate?" She introduces herself as the heir apparent to the Creek chief William Weatherford, and as the young ranger begins to challenge her, we choose to leave them alone for the coming unpleasantness and make our exit. But when we return a few minutes later, they are cooing poetry to each other. Apparently, in the midst of their contention Tumbleweed quoted the opening lines of Byron's "Prisoner of Chillon" ("My hair is gray, but not with years / Nor grew it white / In a single night . . ."), and the ranger—he too a lover of Lord Byron—responded in kind.

Tumbleweed moved to Chicago in 1947. Her late husband, Roscoe Beach, was a teacher and jazz musician, the band master at Martin Luther King High School. She taught the mentally handicapped. Raymond Grossman, now an attorney outside Chicago who Tumbleweed calls "my Jewish son," spent a year teaching with her at Alexander Dumas elementary school on the South Side in 1969, when he was just out of college, living on Martin Luther King Drive. "She was the greatest teacher I've ever seen," he says, her handicapped students testing average for their age-group for the whole school population. "She just reached right into their souls."

She was vice president of the DuSable Museum of African American History, founding its writers' workshop and, after King's assassination, its annual Martinmas Day celebration of King's life, and working throughout at the right hand of the museum's founder, Margaret Burroughs, with whom she maintains a fire-and-ice relationship. "We're not speaking, but that's okay," says Tumbleweed. "We would die for each other."

A few months later, at a gathering at Chicago State University on King Drive after Gwendolyn Brooks's funeral, Burroughs nods wearily at the mention of Tumbleweed. As for Brooks, says Tumbleweed, "Her husband and I were close as razor blades, but she didn't like me, she just didn't like me." Still, Brooks is her favorite poet after Countee Cullen, and Lord Byron. "God kissed that woman," she declares.

In addition to her poetry, from the time she was thirteen and wrote a weekly column, datelined Selma, for the *Pittsburgh Courier*, then among the most widely read black newspapers in the country, Tumbleweed also worked as a journalist. In Chicago she was a founder of the *Woodlawn Observer*, the publication of the activist Woodlawn Organization. Beyond her own writing she was, according to the poet Sterling Plumpp, godmother to countless other black artists and

writers, her home an informal salon. When she moved back to Selma, Plumpp asked her to send him two dollars "so then every black writer in Chicago would owe her money."

Tumbleweed's daughter, Carolyn Delores Beach Foucher, known as Polly, was a nurse and also a Black Panther under the leadership of Bobby Rush. Tumbleweed became a mentor, den mother, bail bondsman, and archivist to the Chicago Panthers. "That woman opened the world to me," says Rush, now a congressman from the South Side.

She played much the same role in the heyday of the American Indian protest movement in Chicago in the early 1970s. "She worked the news media, fund-raising, securing bond. She also gave me the run of her home," says Ben Chosa of the Lac du Flambeau Band of Lake Superior Chippewa. Chosa, a leader in the movement then and now a walleye fishing guide in northern Wisconsin, has been down to Selma to see her.

In 1990 Polly died of cancer. At the funeral, Bobby Rush read from Corinthians; Earl Calloway, the arts editor of the Chicago *Defender*, sang; Margaret Burroughs delivered the eulogy, and H. Rap Brown, by then Jamil Abdullah Al-Amin, spoke. (In 2000, when Al-Amin was being sought for the murder of a sheriff's deputy in Atlanta for which he was ultimately convicted, he fled to the countryside outside Selma and, when he was caught, called J. L. Chestnut to represent him.) Sterling Plumpp read a poem he had written, "Panther Finder (for Polly)": "Them old blues you got tumbling from a Tumbleweed. A wind song jumping from a hurricane."

With the wind song gone, the hurricane blew back to Selma.

On September 12, 2000, Perkins defeats Smitherman.

Joanne Bland, the curator of the Voting Rights Museum, who grew up in the George Washington Carver homes, the projects, on what is now MLK, was driving with a friend onto Broad Street, the main street downtown, just after the polls closed. The car radio wasn't working, so they didn't hear the announcement that Smitherman had been defeated. They didn't need a radio. It seemed

Dorothy Marzette at Get Out the Vote rally the weekend before Selma elected its first black mayor, Ronnie Sharp Park, September 2000

that every black person in Selma poured out onto Broad. "There was a sound so loud you couldn't even hear it, but you could see from the crowd what had happened," says Bland. "We just stopped and got out, I fell." A minister caught her. "I was going to faint. I went to my knees."

For Bland, a big woman with a husky laugh and a withering stare, either of which can be employed at any moment, the only joy that compares was what she felt when she was a twelve-year-old, back in 1965, at the reception the Selma marchers received when they finally made it to Montgomery. Bland and her sister, Linda Lowery, three years older, first saw King at a mass meeting at a Selma church years earlier. They were excited when their grandmother told them she was going to take them to see "King" because they thought she was talking about the Siberian husky from their favorite TV show, *Sergeant Preston of the Yukon*. When they got to church, they were disappointed, until King began to speak.

Bland and Lowery were on the bridge Bloody Sunday. When the police charged the marchers, Lowery was hit in the head, requiring twenty-four stitches in back and eight over her eye. Bland saw a woman trampled by a horse and fainted.

Smitherman was mayor at the time, and for Bland his defeat in 2000 was cathartic. "It was like liberation. I had to go up to the bridge where I had stood all those days with that darn 'Joe Gotta Go' sign and yell, 'Joe is gone.' "

The delirium of celebration on the streets of Selma lasts until morning.

Tumbleweed's phone starts ringing with excited phone calls from friends around the country. When she tells them she was with Joe, they are dumbfounded. She had, after all, been one of the organizers of artists and writers for Harold Washington, who in 1983, in the most triumphant political moment in black Chicago history, was elected the city's first black mayor.

John Hope Franklin calls. He doesn't ask Tumbleweed why she voted for Joe, but she offers a few words of explanation. There came a time in Chicago when she voted for a black candidate over a better white candidate. "It felt wrong," she says. "I told God that if he forgave me I would never vote race again. I'm bored with race."

Less than a month after the election, a monument to Nathan Bedford Forrest, the Confederate general and founder of the Ku Klux Klan, suddenly appears outside the Joseph T. Smitherman Historic Building, a city-owned museum of Confederate artifacts, and the city is again consumed in conflict. On Martin Luther King Day 2001, protesters led by Rose Sanders lasso the five-ton monument and try to pull it down. It doesn't budge.

Martin Luther King and Jeff Davis, Selma

Tumbleweed thinks it would make more sense to place some sturdy wrought-iron benches next to the monument so people could sit and talk about it. "Most of the people in Selma, white and black, have never had a conversation with each other," she says.

"All people have to have their heroes and symbols," she says. "To attempt to take them away is to make an enemy."

At the end of February 2001, with one white councilor crossing racial lines to break the deadlock, the council votes to move the statue to a private cemetery.

The trouble with her people, says Tumbleweed, is that they are both too bothered by other people's symbols and too readily beguiled by their own, like the Martin Luther King Street she lives on.

"All those damn streets are in the black neighborhood," she says. "No matter where you go in this country, there's a Martin Luther King street or drive or place or avenue. I say they still get us with trinkets. We go cheap. I resent it."

Chapter 5

The Soul

Mississippi, Mississippi, Mississippi.
Whether you be heaven or hell, I am here.

Jolivette Anderson, The Poet Warrior,
"Medgar's Last Words"

W here does the soul reside?

Nobody knows. But if you map the soul of black folks, it's got to be somewhere in Mississippi. Got to be. Highest concentration of black people in the United States. Black life and culture everywhere in America are rooted in the South, and this is where the roots run deepest, the blood runs thickest. It is the source, the South's South, the place of longest memories, darkest shadows, whitest whites and bluest blues.

"Mississippi goddamn," Charles Tisdale sums it up, quoting Nina Simone in his resonant rumble. Tisdale is the venerable editor of the *Jackson Advocate*, the black newspaper in Mississippi's capital and largest city.

But just reading those last four words, you've already got the wrong idea. As Akil Bakari at the Malcolm X Grassroots Center on Martin Luther King Drive puts it, "Jackson is just a big old country town." And King Drive is just a big old country road. It meanders a bit and doesn't seem to accomplish a lot, at least in terms of getting you anywhere other than where you already are. You drive by the Drummer house on the corner of King and Scott—in a nondescript rental

Johnny Mack Brown, Jackson, Mississippi

car—just once after being gone a year and a half and when you finally get around to dropping by, Beola Drummer says, "I saw you were in town."

Malcolm X Center

From the outside, the Malcolm X Center on Martin Luther King is a small, dark fortress. In the body language of buildings, this one says, "I am black. Don't mess with me."

The center was founded in the early 1990s after the police killing of a black man who was trying to clean drugs out of one of the local projects. "We didn't choose the street because it was Martin Luther King, but we're happy that it was Martin Luther King," says Chokwe Lumumba, the activist and attorney who founded the center.

Lumumba came to Jackson from Detroit in the early 1970s as part of the Republic of New Afrika, a movement to create a black nation out of five southern states. "My first reaction was, Hell, I want Detroit," he says. That is where the RNA was born. But the movement was drawn inexorably to Mississippi. "I had always known it would be Mississippi first," the RNA's president, Imari Obadele, wrote in his book, *Free the Land.* "I must confess this was because of what they had done to my people; I must confess it is because of the nameless martyrs calling unto me, soul to soul. I knew—I know—it had to be Mississippi."

The RNA bought some land outside Jackson and proclaimed it El Malik. "That was going to be the capital of the new nation," says Lumumba, who presided over the naming ceremony. But a 1971 raid on the RNA headquarters and residence in Jackson ended in the shooting death of a police officer. Obadele and others went to prison. Lumumba went back to law school in Detroit, and after sojourns in Chicago and New York, he returned to Jackson to live in 1988. "It is the center of the problem," he says, and the place he feels most at home, most challenged, and, he has found, most happy raising a family. Still a revolutionary nationalist—he has chaired the New Afrikan People's Organization since its founding in 1984—Lumumba has also emerged as a very successful attorney, taking on some of the most sensational, racially charged cases in Mississippi and elsewhere. Long, lean, and casually dashing, Lumumba conveys something compelling and disarming as he traverses the very different worlds of radical black aspirations and turn-of-the-twenty-first-century Mississippi reality with equal aplomb.

Inside, the Malcolm X Center is a place for classes and lectures, for summer camp, for the New Afrikan Scouts, a national group whose first president was the late rapper Tupac Shakur, whom Lumumba represented in one scrape after another, most famously at a preliminary hearing at the courthouse on MLK in Atlanta when Shakur was charged with shooting two off-duty Atlanta police officers. The charges were later dropped.

The Malcolm X Center is also home to the Jackson Panthers, their very successful basketball team, which in recent years have been state champs more often than not. Every spring, Lumumba runs the Black History Classic tournament for teams from throughout the South. "I've reclaimed my interest in sports since I've been down here," he says. "Back in the seventies I wouldn't have been bouncing no basketball. I would have been at the rifle range."

Lumumba says that when he and others from the Republic of New Afrika showed up in Jackson's black community thirty years ago, "a lot of folks were fascinated by us, but they didn't feel we were them. Now, we are them."

Lanier High School

In 1931 a mathematician by the name of Kurt Gödel posited a groundbreaking theorem that there are statements in mathematics that are true but could never be proven true mathematically, and he could prove it.

In 1960 Robert Moses, a math teacher from Harlem with a master's in philosophy from Harvard, was spending his summer working as a volunteer at the Southern Christian Leadership Conference office in Atlanta when he attended a lecture, "Ramifications of Gödel's Theorem," at Atlanta University (it later merged with Clark College on what is now Atlanta's MLK Drive). At the lecture, Moses heard that the Southern Conference Educational Fund was going to be picketing in support of a planned department store sit-in. As he recounts the

episode in his book, *Radical Equations: Math Literacy and Civil Rights*, on his way to the picketing Moses was picked up by police. Later he was called into Martin Luther King's study at Ebenezer Baptist Church, where King gently cautioned him that, fairly or not, the SCEF had been investigated for Communist links. "We have to be careful," King told Moses.

For the six years to follow, Moses, without ego, angels, or the remotest odds of success, but with enormous care and incalculable courage, disappeared into the wilds of Mississippi and mobilized the voting rights movement that lit a fire in what he had described in a note he wrote in 1961 from the county jail in Magnolia as "the middle of the iceberg." Gone from Mississippi for a quarter century—in Canada, teaching math in Tanzania, and getting his doctorate in the philosophy of math at Harvard—he returned in 1992, and returns most weeks since, commuting from his home in Cambridge, Massachusetts, to Jackson— flying in each Monday and flying out at week's end—to deliver personally, now with the help of three of his grown children, the national Algebra Project he created to free young black people from the modern serfdom of math illiteracy. First it was Jackson's Brinkley Middle School, and now it's at Lanier High School on King Drive.

Moses remains a Zen blend—intense and gentle, demanding and patient, and always quiet, very quiet but for those searching dark eyes. After a while you begin to wonder if there weren't times when that haunting gaze saved his life.

In his geometry class this day, Moses is asking his students to explain and diagram how the eighteenth-century Scottish mathematician John Playfair arrived at his version of Euclid's postulate 5. Moses crouches next to each student to go over the work. In the back one young man is slouched way low in his chair reading the newspaper, ignoring the entreaty of another student to put it away. Without even looking at him or raising his voice, Moses instructs the student to take his newspaper and chair out into the hallway and come back when he's finished reading and ready to learn.

Robert Moses at Lanier High School. Architect of Freedom Summer and founder of the Algebra Project, Moses commutes each week from Cambridge, Massachusetts, to teach math at Lanier.

In the anteroom in back of the classroom, Jolivette Anderson works in a whisper on Moses's travel schedule. She is his assistant, but she is also the Poet Warrior, a name fitting her do-or-die passions and the rolling, roiling power of her booming laugh.

Anderson was born in Shreveport, Louisiana, months after King's assassination. "I heard the thump of his body when it hit the balcony / even though I was still in my mama's womb," goes a line in a poem on her CD, *At the End of a Rope, In Mississippi*, into which she weaves interviews with Moses, Lumumba, and Tisdale taken from her radio show, *The Mississippi Cipher*.

After school, in the Lanier parking lot, Anderson turns on her car radio. Tisdale is discussing the upcoming state referendum on keeping the Confederate emblem on the Mississippi flag with Richard Barrett, a white supremacist who grew up in New York and New Jersey and moved to Mississippi in 1966. Reprising resentments from thirty and forty years ago, Barrett is flaying the Republic of New Afrika and the Kennedys. Anderson is shaking her head.

Tisdale speaks slowly, his voice hugging the lower registers. When we interviewed him in his office earlier in the week, his eyes were so heavy, so lidded he looked on the verge of sleep. He was not. Tisdale described to us how his career in black newspapers took him from Chicago to Memphis to Jackson, which the way he makes it out, is like tumbling down a flight of stairs.

"Why did I come here? I am confused. Anybody who could escape should do so." Tisdale is not confused. He is ornery; his newspaper's office has been a frequent target of attacks over the years. "If they hadn't tried to run me off, I probably would have left."

We are meeting him thirty-three years and a day since the assassination of King. Tisdale was working in Memphis then for the *Mid-South Times*. On that day a black police officer and black firefighter, both of whom had been suddenly pulled off their duty protecting King, came to Tisdale, worried. "When Martin Luther King was killed we were in a car on our way to warn him that something was wrong. We never got there."

In 1955 Tisdale, then a reporter with the Chicago *Defender*, was in Mississippi for the trial of the two white men who were acquitted—after an hour and eight minutes of deliberation—of the murder of Emmett Till, the fourteen-year-old Chicago boy who was visiting his uncle in Money, Mississippi, when he supposedly whistled at a white woman and ended up shot and drowned. "We stood under a tree because they wouldn't let us in the courtroom at that time. Every morning the sheriff would come by and he would speak to us and I think in his most benevolent tone say, 'Good morning niggers.' "

"I do wonder what keeps me here," Anderson muses. But, like Tisdale, she knows. "The deep spirituality of the place that keeps me grounded. Listening to what the ancestors have to say. The ancestors are saying a whole lot in Mississippi. That's what makes me stay."

Brown's Freeway Service Station

"I'm used to hard times," says W. L. Stokes, a man with a face of abiding eloquence, who grew up picking cotton "from can to can't, from can see to can't see," and now shares his days trading stories and playing pool checkers with the old-timers at Brown's gas station on Jackson's King.

These men, however, lived their lives along the arc from can't to can. They came of age at a time when "nothing and nothing could stop Mississippi," as Gwendolyn Brooks put it in a poem about the death of Emmett Till. Stokes served in the segregated military. Jack Bennett played Negro League ball. Johnny Mack Brown was a Pullman porter when that was about the best job a black man could have. Wardell Catchings broke the color line driving a city bus. Quincy Brown, the proprietor of Brown's, marched for freedom.

They saw it all, survived it all, somehow intact, strong and sweet.

Catchings and Stokes are playing pool checkers on Brown's well-worn red-and-white board. Pool checkers is to checkers what Michael Jordan's game is to James Naismith's. In pool checkers, pieces can jump in either direction, and once kinged can fly over empty spaces, even turning at right angles in midjump. The playing roster at Brown's is an eclectic mix—men in suits, in work jumpers, in overalls, even a former national champ.

"I wouldn't do that if I was you," Stokes, El Producto clenched between his

W. L. Stokes

teeth, tells Catchings, who is gently sliding his piece along. His hand quivers slightly.

"I didn't see that," says Catchings.

"You saw it," replies Stokes, raising and slamming his piece—clack, clack, clack, clack—a quadruple jump. "You're just playing the wrong person. You know who I am, don't you?"

Catchings takes the second match with a quintuple jump. But by the third game, Stokes is back in command. "Go, Tricky Dicky," Stokes says, goading himself to victory. "Go, Tricky Dicky."

Catchings grew up about twenty miles south of Jackson in Crystal Springs. He moved to Jackson at age sixteen, the Tuesday after the third Sunday, August 1948. He knows that because that Sunday was the annual revival at his church,

Checkerboard, Brown's Freeway Service Station

Pool checkers

Bush Creek Baptist. It was so hot, an old man dropped dead in front of him. "They had him on a big old block of ice," recalls Catchings. He decided then and there to leave Crystal Springs. "When I get scared I'm gone. You don't have to scare me a second time."

In 1961 Catchings moved to Los Angeles. Loved it. But on August 11, 1965, the Watts riots began twelve blocks from where he was living. "Thirty-four people killed, snipers, rioters. Sunday night it was over. Soon as the bank opened up Monday morning, I got my money and came back home," he says, figuring, "If I got to fight I'd rather be home." The same day he arrived back in Jackson he was hired as the city's second black bus driver, starting work August 20, 1965. He remembers the first time he drove the bus, people on the route just staring at him. Some whites would not get on. "I'll tell you one thing," one of the old white drivers training him said laughing, "if they see you again they'll damn sure know you." Catchings recalls those trainers fondly. "It seemed like they all felt good about it."

Catchings worked that job for thirty-two years. The other black driver who started just before him did not last very long. Somebody fired shots at his home. "Nothing happened to me," says Catchings. "If they'd fired on my house I'd probably been back in California."

Johnny Mack Brown lives in a well-kept little bright blue house a short walk from Brown's. When we stop by, the Four Tops are on the radio. "I Can't Help Myself (Sugar Pie, Honey Bunch)."

"I'll show you my bedroom," he says. Actually Brown, who is almost eighty-six, has two bedrooms. One, into which the soft afternoon light is streaming, has a framed picture of Jesus bathed in a shaft of light from Heaven above. Brown's other bedroom is darker. An old *Playboy* centerfold is casually pasted on the wall.

Wardell Catchings

On the dresser across the room from his bed is a big boom box. Grabbing the remote from the bed stand, Brown turns the box on and the volume all the way up. The room shakes. Brown beams.

He was a Pullman porter from 1945 to 1975, traveling the length and breadth of America. He married his wife in 1935. She died in 1991. "I must have had the right one," he says, "because I haven't married another one since.

"She liked to see me when I came home. She was sad to see when I leave. She knew she wasn't going to see me for six weeks."

He liked his job all right. He met Harry Truman, Clark Gable, and Roy Rogers and Dale Evans. But he doesn't miss it. "When I was in my forties I was talking about sixty-five. I wanted sixty-five to come."

He paid off his house—it cost four thousand dollars—in 1962. He drives a Chevy Impala with 91,000 miles on it. His health is excellent. "Soul food keeps you going. Chicken wings, rice with gravy, butter rolls, liver."

Brown has the beatific countenance of a blues saint. "Jazz is my favorite, but most women want to hear blues, they don't want to hear the jazz. I wonder why."

A tall young woman stops by to use the telephone. After she leaves, Brown explains the phone call was a pretext—she is really trying to get close to him. It is a statement we would not have found credible an hour earlier.

Brown's prayer: "If You're going to send me someone for my girlfriend, let it be one of the best ones You made.

"I've had my fun," he says. "I'm well acquainted with life. I got it made."

The Drummers

A few doors up from Brown's house, at the corner of MLK and Scott, is the home of Beola Drummer.

A piece of paper taped on the front door says, "No Public Restrooms. Don't even Ask!!!!!!!"

It's a joke of sorts. People are constantly in and out of the house, children

Johnny Mack Brown

Beola Drummer

dropped off and picked up, food simmering on the stove. On our first visit, a woman sits on the porch enjoying a long drink of iced tea. When she leaves, we ask who she was. Drummer shrugs, smiles. When Drummer won big at bingo, she bought two large plastic swimming pools for the neighborhood kids to splash in. She still helps the elderly couple she used to live next door to do their shopping.

Drummer provides a running commentary on life. She snaps off a tree branch and, as she strips off the stems and leaves, riffs on the glory of switches. "This is good for potty training. This is good for people who don't know when to shut their mouth. This is the key to everything." She has four children, three of whom have already graduated from Lanier, the fourth, Jessica, coming up.

Lanier High School Prom/Black History Classic Basketball Tournament

Jessica Drummer cleans house on prom day.

Chokwe Lumumba's Black History Classic and the Lanier High School prom are the same weekend in April 2001.

The tournament is held at several Jackson public schools and Tougaloo College, a historic black school on the edge of town where Lumumba's daughter, Rukia, is the reigning Miss Tougaloo. The prom is held at the Crowne Plaza Downtown.

Jessica Drummer gets ready for the prom with the help of her sisters.

While the prom is all black, the tournament has a few white players. There are white Panthers. The loudest-mouthed fan at the tournament is the father of a white Panther. The Panthers' slick souvenir booklet, underwritten by Adidas, includes a detailed recounting of the revolutionary history of the Panther name and congratulatory ads from McDonald's, several banks, and the local power company.

"We're nationalists, not separatists," says Lumumba. He embroiders a little black nationalism into a morning pep talk for all the tournament players that is mostly intended to encourage them to stay on top of their academics. "So we say, 'free the land,' " he says. "In life, we are all on the same side in the mighty struggle against oppression."

Lanier High School prom

Attorney Chokwe Lumumba coaches the Jackson Panthers, Black History Classic, Tougaloo College.

Girls compete to be elected Lanier's prom queen. Fareeda Figgers's campaign posters were especially memorable: "I have a dream . . . to be your prom queen."

Prom night, as Fareeda dresses, her father, Frank, takes us outside to show us something. The Figgerses live on a small street that connects King Drive and Medgar Evers Boulevard, not far from where Evers, then state director of the NAACP, was shot to death in the driveway of his home in 1963. From his yard, Figgers points to the homes where he and his wife, Laura, grew up, where their grandparents lived. "It was a lot of family right around," says Laura. "We could almost throw a rock at each other."

A cousin used to live next door. He was the cartoonist for the NAACP newsletter. "The night they killed Medgar Evers somebody threw a brick through their window," says Frank Figgers. "It said, 'You're next.' He loaded up and moved that night." Never came back.

Down King at the Drummers', Jessica (nickname Jesse) is in her room primping for the prom. The sign on her door says: KEEP OUT! AJA & JESSE ONLY. KEEP MY DOOR CLOSED, MY TV OFF. DO NOT SIT ON MY PILLOWS (IF I LET YOU IN). IF I AIN'T HERE YOU SHOULDN'T BE HERE NEITHER. RESPECT MY PROPERTY AS YOU WOULD YO' MAMMY!

Aja is Jessica's baby daughter. Jessica's sister, who lives nearby, has a baby, KeSean, with W. L. Stokes's great-grandson, who is away at medical school. The baby's grandfather, Kenneth, is the city councilor responsible for getting this street named for King and for the ebullient King Day parade that ends as it passes the Drummer front porch.

A neighbor—a transvestite who goes to his job as a nurse dressed as a woman—was supposed to do Jessica's hair for the prom, but he was called to work. A secretary at Lanier fills in, and lends Jessica her boyfriend's car for the night. Cinderella had nothing on Jessica.

As she irons Jessica's powder blue satin prom dress, Beola Drummer is reminiscing about "the laziest dog in the world," the one that put its paws over its eyes to avoid the light, that had to be dragged on its walks, that would give you this look like "if you want that damn stick you better get it yourself.

"This dog was lazy!"

Outside, Mississippi is spread wide against the night, but inside, the house is tiny, cramped, and worn. The Drummers are poor, and fortunate. Here, in the soul of black America, Beola Drummer is a good soul. Of growing up in Laurel, Mississippi, she has eerie memories of cross burnings and Klansmen waving from a passing train. When Jessica was eight, Beola's nephew held the family hostage, at gunpoint, here at the house. (He is now on Mississippi death row for the contract murder of a pregnant woman.) But she does not dwell on such memories. "Life's too short to be sad," says Drummer. "I enjoy life."

Canton

We follow Chokwe Lumumba twenty minutes north of Jackson to Canton, where in that cloistered little town's prosaic new courthouse, he is defending a

Safe house, Canton, Mississippi. In 1966 Clarece Coney opened her home to Martin Luther King, Jr., Stokely Carmichael, and some 135 other civil rights marchers when they were tear-gassed by police on the Memphis-to-Jackson march while attempting to camp across the street.

man accused of robbing and killing a woman at her antique shop in Yazoo City. A couple of blocks away is Canton's grand old Greek Revival courthouse. It, and the graceful square that surrounds it, are so small-town Southern picture perfect they could be a movie set. And so they are, with credits that include *My Dog Skip, O Brother, Where Art Thou?* and John Grisham's *A Time to Kill,* in which a black father who kills the white men who raped his ten-year-old daughter is tried for murder amid the racial passions of a town much like Canton.

On this last movie, the first filmed in Canton, the local woman coordinating the extras was Clarece Coney, who found herself making several very cameo appearances in the movie. "One of the main scenes was a courtroom scene where I was crying and everybody asked me how did I cry, me not being an actress." Coney's method may have something to do with her having lived through Canton's racial tribulations, a drama in which she had a much larger part. In fact, Coney's home, located near the corner of what is now Martin Luther King Avenue and George Washington Avenue (this George Washington was a generous local black businessman), was the setting for an indelible moment in the life of Canton and King.

In June 1966, James Meredith, who in 1962 had integrated Ole Miss, undertook a solo March Against Fear from Memphis to Jackson. The second day out, he was shot, and other civil rights leaders, including Martin Luther King and Stokely Carmichael, took up where Meredith left off. It was to be the march on which Carmichael first led a crowd to chant "Black Power," to King's great discomfort. When the march, gathering force along the way, reached Canton, they planned to camp on the grounds of the black school across from Coney's house. The police, however, decided that was not to be. When the marchers would not disperse, they tear-gassed the crowd and cleared the fields, billy clubs swinging. In their retreat, many of the marchers took refuge in Coney's home.

"I had 137 people here at my house," she recalls. "They were packed in like sardines. Stokely Carmichael was stretched out on my front porch." King came, comforting and calming people.

As we are driving out of town along MLK, we come upon another classic Mississippi tableau. A man in his prison stripes is tending the monkey grass outside a book storage facility. His name is James Talbert. He tells us about how he got started dealing drugs in the army and kept at it on his return home to Hattiesburg, Mississippi. He didn't use drugs, only sold them, more and more blatantly, until he finally got caught. "I just stood there," he says, explaining that he needed saving. His time is almost up, and he is determined to make good on his release. "Hell is real. I do believe in that," he says. "I don't want none of that. You think the sun is hot."

Dominos. Center, Texas.

Chapter 6

The Heart

we are not a tribe
we are a nation.
we are not wandering groups
we are a people.

Haki R. Madhubuti, "Life Poems"

Chicago's Martin Luther King Drive is colder in every way than its country cousin in Jackson, Mississippi. It's a big, broad, bricks-and-mortar straight shot through the South Side as far as the eye can see. Stretches are grand. Patches are worn. But if it angled just a hair west and kept south for another 749 miles, it would run right back into the King Drive in Jackson. And then the truth would become apparent: The two streets are connected by everything but tar and macadam, connected like before is to after, "what about" is to "you don't say," motherland is to colony, and soul is to everlasting soul.

High up along a noble expanse of Martin Luther King Drive in a part of Chicago's South Side known as Bronzeville is a beautiful statue in bronze by the sculptor Alison Saar dedicated to the Great Northern Migration. It's a man both jaunty and sad, his back facing south toward Mississippi, arriving with a suitcase tied with string, wearing a suit made up of shoe soles.

Monument to the Great Northern Migration, Bronzeville, Chicago

Martin Luther King Drive

"I'm going to the sweetest place in the world, that cool breeze blowing on the Michigan Lake. Everybody's happy and there's no more heartache," Sam Theard sang in 1938. "You ask, they call it heaven, but it's South Park Way."

South Park Way is now Martin Luther King Drive.

"When I got off at the train station, I saw all the lights and things, it was like entering paradise," says Rose Marie Black, who arrived in 1946 at age twelve from Summit, Mississippi.

When we first catch sight of her, Black is a vision in white—thigh-high boots, skirt up to here, hat out to there. We are driving south on King Drive, and Black is about to board a northbound bus. She must be used to the sound of screeching brakes, the swiveling salute of turned heads. She is Racetrack Rosie, the Bronze Temptress—at sixty-six, Chicago's oldest stripper.

("The one with the hat out to there?" asks Jack Bennett, back at Brown's gas station on the MLK in Jackson when we recollect our encounter with Black. After playing Negro League ball, Bennett spent the shank of his life working for the post office in Chicago before coming home to Mississippi.)

In the upstream geography of black America, Mississippi is the source and Chicago the Delta. If Mississippi locates the soul in the metaphysical body that is the poet Haki Madhubuti's black nation, then Chicago must be something like its beating heart, a pulsing vital center, the chosen home of Jesse Jackson and Louis Farrakhan, of *Ebony* and *Jet*, of Michael Jordan when he ruled the world, and Oprah in her reign. Muddy Waters and Willie Dixon were Mississippi-born and Chicago-mourned, their funerals on King. As the poet Gwendolyn Brooks described it at the 1983 inauguration of the city's first black mayor, Harold Washington, Chicago is the "I Will city . . . ripe / roused / ready: / richly rambunctious, implausible: / sudden, or saddle-steady."

It is poetic justice, Chicago style, that Brooks's last public act—the last time she left her home before she died in December 2000—was to vote in that November's election. And as Madhubuti tells us when we see him at Brooks's wake, "She didn't go out to vote for Bush."

We spend the days surrounding Election Day 2000 on Martin Luther King Drive in Chicago, the most political of days on the most political of ways.

"To be apolitical is to be political in a negative way for black-folks," Madhubuti wrote in his 1969 book, *Don't Cry, Scream*, back before he traded the simplicity of his given name—Don L. Lee—for a mouthful of Swahili meaning. Madhubuti was referring to the politics inherent to black art. But the same goes for all aspects of black expression. There is no avoiding politics if you are black in America. The very meaning of what it is to be black in America has always been defined by law, determined by politics.

"You know, actually all that I do on civil rights I do because I consider it part of my ministry," King sermonized at Mount Pisgah Missionary Baptist Church on what is now MLK in August 1967, in the last throes of his rocky effort to bring the movement north by way of Chicago.

On Election Day 2000, the Martin Luther King Center at Mount Pisgah is a polling place. Across MLK at Liberty Baptist on the Sunday before, the third-generation pastor Darrell L. Jackson, a Morehouse man, makes it plain from the pulpit: "You use your vote on Tuesday. I'm not telling you how, but I'm not voting for no Bush. I didn't vote for his daddy and I'm not voting for him. I'm voting for Gore."

The front page of the election week issue of the *Chicago Crusader* is dominated by the newspaper's endorsements, beginning with Al Gore. Below that is the editor Shirley Lester's interview with the sister of James Byrd, who in 1998 was picked up on the MLK we will visit in Jasper, Texas, and dragged to death in the most notorious lynching of recent times. The headline: "Sister of hate crime victim says: A 'yes' vote for Bush is a 'no' vote for Blacks." Another front-page headline alerts readers to a story on page 3: "Bush Family Allegedly Linked to Nazis."

Inside, an editorial cartoon depicts Bush as a bloodthirsty wolf in sheep's clothing, tracking "death row blood." "The Chatterbox" gossip column, bylined Ima Gontellit, warns that, if Bush gets in the White House, "it will be wholesale warfare on the Black community." An NAACP get-out-the-vote ad quotes James Byrd's daughter: "My father was dragged three miles behind a truck until his life was taken from him. Hate crimes must be put to an end."

The *Chicago Crusader*, located on an aimless stretch of MLK, is less famous than the Chicago *Defender*, which was, in effect, the official paper of the Great Migration, circulating south, summoning blacks north. But, says Dorothy Leavell, the *Crusader's* spirited publisher, "I think we are more militant than they are." The *Crusader* motto—"Blacks Must Control Their Own Community"—appears above the masthead and on the bottom of every page. Celebrating its sixtieth year, the paper began as a newsletter for a black labor organization. Leavell, who grew up in Pine Bluff, Arkansas, is the widow of its cofounder, Balm L. Leavell, Jr.

Lester, the editor, went from high school to the air force and then, returning to Chicago, got a job working for the attorney Benjamin C. Duster. He is the grandson of Ida B. Wells-Barnett, the Mississippi-born antilynching crusader and journalist who lived on what is now MLK and for whom Chicago's first all-black housing project, edging King, is named.

Lester says Duster was bothered that someone as smart as she had not gone to college. "He couldn't rest until I was in college, enrolled." He called Dolores Cross, then the president of Chicago State University, a mostly black public college on King, and later president of Morris Brown College on Atlanta's MLK when we spent Freshman Week there. At Chicago State, Lester became editor of the student paper, a thorn in the administration's side. "I was viewed at the school as a problem," she brags. "That's exactly what I was."

We are waiting for Lu Palmer outside the rickety house that is home to the independent black political operation he founded. It is located on Lu Palmer

Mattie Walker votes at Turner Memorial Church, Election Day 2000.

Place, just up from the corner with King Drive. While we are waiting, an old man shambles by, not terribly well dressed. It is Palmer. He is seventy-eight and, we learn later, barely able to see. He looks like Ulysses, home from the Odyssey, disguised as an old beggar and awaiting the moment when he will reveal himself and smite the suitors trying to make time with his wife while he has been away. In fact, Palmer and his ailing wife, Jorja, live at the corner of Lu Palmer and King in a forty-room castle—turrets, howling wind, and all.

Palmer is revered in black Chicago—for his writing, his newspaper columns, his radio show, his willingness to quit or be fired whenever one of his various employers over the years tried to shut him up for being too outspokenly black, and for his impresario's role in producing the climactic moment in modern black political history, the 1983 election of Harold Washington as mayor.

It was in the castle basement that Palmer and a handful of others persuaded the reluctant Washington to make the run. "My wife served watermelon and we were strategizing and kicking Harold's butt."

For twelve years Palmer had been delivering personal political commentary on *Lu's Notebook*, which ran on all four of Chicago's black radio stations. "You couldn't miss me." The show was sponsored by Illinois Bell, which would periodically try to cancel it, only to relent in the face of black community pressure. "Most black people long to talk about white people bad." But the same morning that Washington announced for mayor, Illinois Bell finally did cancel *Lu's Notebook*. "They said, 'You have been too outspoken in pushing Harold Washington.' So they fired me."

Lutrelle Palmer grew up in Newport News, Virginia. His father was the principal of Huntington High School, a black school with an exceptional reputation. Palmer says that after pouring his heart into the school for twenty-three years, his father was fired on trumped-up charges of being a Communist. He died a broken man.

As was the practice at the time, the state of Virginia paid for Palmer's graduate education in communications at the University of Iowa so they would not

Lu Palmer

have to admit a black student to the University of Virginia. Palmer came to Chicago to work on his doctoral dissertation—a content analysis of the *Defender*. He was soon working there.

In his more than a decade with the *Defender*, Palmer quit three times. "There was just no sense of mission and I just couldn't deal with it," he explains. He crossed over to the "white press"—the old *Chicago American*. "I didn't last long there because the racism was so intense." He went to the *Chicago Daily News*, and by the late 1960s he had his own column, "somebody to color the city from a black perspective." But, he says, he colored it too black. "They would tinker with my columns and sometimes refuse to run them and it just became unbearable."

In January 1973 he called a press conference and quit. "I said flat out that any black reporter who works for a white newspaper is not a black reporter." He started his own newspaper, refusing white advertisements. It lasted fourteen months.

Since 1983 he has had a talk radio show. (He retired in January 2001.) He is on the air until midnight election night, ringing in the historically inconclusive results, denouncing both Bush and Gore as bad for blacks. (He voted for Nader.) "I say we can't depend on either party."

He considered himself a disciple of Martin Luther King in his lifetime but now believes King was wrong about two things—nonviolence and integration. "The worst thing to ever happen to black people was integration."

Palmer's castle is broken up into apartments, but renting them has become a losing game—"drugs and all of that foolishness you just don't want to contend with."

There is something both heroic and forlorn about Palmer, devoting himself so wholly to his people, trying to maintain a castle on King.

Four blocks north of Palmer's castle on King Drive is the stately Griffin Funeral Home, from where they buried Jesse Owens and Elijah Muhammad and where, each morning, they raise to half-mast a Confederate flag (along with an American flag, a black freedom flag, and a POW flag). It is a practice begun in 1990 by the late owner, Ernest Griffin, when he learned that his mortuary stood on the site of Camp Douglas, a notorious prisoner-of-war camp where more than six thousand Confederate soldiers died. Remarkably, it turned out that, before it was a prison, the camp was a Union training and induction center where Griffin's own grandfather enlisted in the U.S. Colored Infantry during the Civil War. Griffin devoted the last years of his life to the study of Civil War history, going south to appear before meetings of the Sons of Confederate Veterans. His funeral home has become a place of personal pilgrimage for the descendants of those Confederate dead who have heard about the black funeral home on King Drive that daily pays its respects.

"I have literally seen prejudices dissipate," says James O'Neal, Griffin's son-in-law, who continues his father-in-law's work. He recalls coming to work one morning to find a white man curled up in a van in the parking lot. The van had Michigan plates, but the young man had a deep Southern drawl and said he had

Harold Newchurch raises the Confederate flag at Griffin Funeral Home. The funeral home is located on the site of a notorious POW camp where more than six thousand Confederate soldiers died.

Rose Marie Black, a.k.a. Racetrack Rosie, the Bronze Temptress

lost a great-great-grandfather there. "You could tell by his demeanor that he did not wish to be in the middle of an African American community, so I said, 'Do you know your ancestor's name?' 'Yeah.' He was very belligerent, 'Yeah!' I said, 'Just a second.' " O'Neal brought the man inside to meet his father-in-law. "I said, 'Dad, this gentleman lost his ancestor.' Dad talked to the young man, found his ancestor's name in the book of all the casualties, and talked to him for twenty minutes," says O'Neal. "When that young man left here he had a smile on his face, a change of heart, and you could tell that his demeanor had reshaped itself."

"Sometimes when I'm standing on the corner with my short skirt a guy will say, 'How much?' I say, 'Ask your mamma.' Oh yes, I have an answer, honey." This is Rose Marie Black, the day after we first met her, now at the White Castle on Stoney Island Avenue, a favorite haunt. This time, Black is a vision in black and white, another eye-popping outfit of her own creation. She is brimming with street sense.

"I've been married thirty-two miserable years. There is no love in the marriage. He knows that. I even told his mother. She wanted to know why I would stay with someone I didn't love. Because he pays the bills," she says. "I do have a boyfriend because I believe in two of everything. Didn't you notice the good Lord gave you two of everything—two eyebrows, two eyes, two nostrils, two lips, two arms, two legs."

Black does not drink or use drugs and is mostly vegetarian. "I'm high on cod-liver oil and vitamins."

The secret of life: "Peace of mind, and the key to peace of mind is gratitude to God." The secret of stripping: "Always leave something to the imagination."

On politics: "Anybody that don't vote, honey, is in deep trouble with me. What president you voting for? If you say Bush, you'd be in trouble."

Bobby Rush, the former Black Panther, is now a congressman and, just as important here, the Democratic committeeman for the Second Ward with an office in a strip mall on MLK next to Mississippi Rick's takeout. Inside the office there are pictures of Rush and Harold Washington blown up so large you can count the men's pores. Rush votes at little Turner Memorial Church, which looks more deep-country Mississippi than South Side Chicago.

Outside Turner, Aaron "Stoney Burke" Johnson greets voters with cool proficiency. He is the superintendent of transportation for the Chicago Post Office. (Of course, Jack Bennett back at Brown's in Jackson knows Stoney.) He is also the local Democratic precinct captain.

Johnson is wearing a cowboy hat. He has mandarin-long fingernails. His nickname is borrowed from a rodeo cowboy played by Jack Lord on a short-lived 1962 TV series. Johnson rides a horse down MLK in the annual Bud

Billiken Parade, the largest black parade in America, founded and sponsored by the Chicago *Defender*.

We explain our mission, and start to describe Rose Marie Black. Johnson excuses himself to retrieve something from his car. He returns with photocopies of newspaper stories about Black. He is the boyfriend she told us about.

Johnson also has some clippings about himself. In 1982 readers of the Chicago *Defender* voted him the Most Sensational Man in Chicago. The runners-up, in order, were a Baptist preacher, the city's assistant superintendent of streets and sewers, the manager of a South Side Church's Fried Chicken restaurant, another Baptist preacher, and the Reverend Jesse Jackson. According to a *Defender* story ("What makes Stoney so sensational?"), Johnson owed his victory to his "personality" and a very big vote coming out of the post office.

When Johnson delivers his precinct tallies to Rush's ward office election night, Gore defeats Bush, 352 to 10, and Johnson knew about those 10 going in.

When we visit Haki Madhubuti at noon on Election Day, he has already tried to vote but the lines were too long. He will vote later.

Madhubuti is a professor at Chicago State University, where, with Dolores Cross when she was president, he saw to the creation of the Gwendolyn Brooks Center with an annual writers' conference and hall of fame for writers of African descent and a professorship for Brooks.

"What does a son do for a mother?" asks Madhubuti, who came to Chicago from Arkansas by way of Detroit. He says Brooks saved and softened him.

He is a prolific and popular poet and essayist, "an interpreter and protector of Blackness," in Brooks's words, having emerged, when he was known as Don Lee, as one of the sharpest figures of the black arts movement of the 1960s. His 1990 book, *Black Men: Obsolete, Single, Dangerous?*, has remained a bestseller in black bookstores.

In 1987 he wrote about himself, in the third person, in *Poet: What Ever Happened to Luther?*—Luther being the middle name he shared with MLK: "he was into that black stuff and he was as light skinned as a piece of golden corn on the

Aaron "Stoney Burke" Johnson, Democratic precinct captain, at Turner Memorial Church, Election Day 2000

cob." So light skinned that in 1974 he decided to take a name as black as his consciousness—Haki, which in Swahili means "just," and Madhubuti, "precise" or "accurate."

He says his commitment to black people is "as serious as first love." Serious is right. There is nothing giddy about Madhubuti's romance with blackness. He has devoted his life to building independent black institutions on the South Side. He has founded two Afrocentric schools—a public charter school and a private preschool—and, beginning in 1967 in a basement apartment, Third World Press. The publishing house, a mainstay of black intellectual life nationally, now occupies a former Catholic rectory with the quiet and class of some well-appointed Ivy League foundation.

Madhubuti speaks in muffled, measured tones. He has presence or, as we find traveling on King, omnipresence. He seems to have been everywhere, as profoundly influential in black America as he is invisible to the rest of America.

In 1989, when students occupied the administration building at Morris Brown College on MLK in Atlanta, they called Madhubuti for advice. In 1995 Madhubuti brokered a historic peace between the Nation of Islam's Louis Farrakhan and Betty Shabazz, the widow of Malcolm X, that was publicly sealed at the Apollo Theater on MLK in Harlem and broadcast to a closed-circuit audience around the world.

When Jolivette Anderson, the poet we met at Lanier High School on MLK in Jackson, wrote her book-length poem about a freedom tour she was helping to lead when the bus plunged into a river, killing a close friend and stealing her voice for a year, she sent the manuscript to Madhubuti. Unbidden, without ever talking to her, he returned the manuscript along with a beautiful introduction he had written for it.

Election night the wind is rustling along MLK. There seems a chill of foreboding that Bush will prevail. "Straight, straight, straight, straight," a woman cries out in front of the polling place at Mount Pisgah. She is urging a straight Democratic vote. Bush's ancestors, she says, owned her ancestors. The corners of a Rainbow/PUSH Coalition handbill, slapped on a lamppost, flap in the breeze. It bears a photo of a young Jesse Jackson leaning over Martin Luther King. "Learn about the power of voting from a King," it says.

On December 3, Gwendolyn Brooks dies at home, Madhubuti by her side. She is buried in the snowbound South Side. She is waked at A. A. Rayner & Sons Funeral Home, a block and a half off MLK on East Seventy-first, also known as Emmett Till Road.

In the summer of 1955, they waked Till, the fourteen-year-old Chicago boy murdered in Money, Mississippi, while visiting family. His mother insisted on an open coffin so the world could see her son's grotesquely mutilated body. A photo

Haki Madhubuti in his office at Third World Press

"Have a Dream" mural

of Till in his casket, published in *Jet*, remains among the most indelible images of African American history, the distilled essence of what white Americans were capable of doing to black Americans. *Jet* reported that hundreds of thousands of mourners "in an unending procession" filed by Till's coffin.

Brooks wrote "The Last Quatrain of the Ballad of Emmett Till (After the Murder, After the Burial)."

> She kisses her killed boy.
> And she is sorry.
> Chaos in windy grays
> through a red prairie.

The white men charged with killing Till were acquitted after a dramatic trial and perfunctory deliberations. "One of the most important factors accounting for the difference between the Negro in Chicago and the Negro in Money,

Miss.," the *Defender* editorialized after the verdict, "is that the Negro in Chicago can and does vote."

"Emmett Till's name is a boomerang calling black maleness," Sterling Plumpp, the Chicago poet out of Clinton and Jackson, Mississippi, who is at Brooks's wake, writes in a poem of tribute on her death. Thirty years earlier, Madhubuti brought Plumpp to meet Brooks at her home, bleak but for its books and books. She paid out of her own pocket to publish Plumpp's first book of poetry.

Plumpp introduces us to Lerone Bennett, the executive editor of *Ebony* magazine and an important historian of the black experience, who, sharp and lithe, presides over Brooks's funeral the next day. In 1945 Bennett graduated from Lanier High School in Jackson and went off to Morehouse College, where he was a year behind King.

"Did you know he had something?" we ask.

"I knew that everybody at Morehouse had something," Bennett replies. "Yeah, I knew that everybody did."

Chapter 7

Late Word of Freedom

"The people of Texas are informed that in accordance with a Proclamation from the Executive of the United States, all slaves are free. This involves an absolute equality of rights and rights of property between former masters and slaves, and the connection heretofore existing between them becomes between employer and hired labor. The Freedmen are advised to remain at their present homes and work for wages. They are informed that they will not be allowed to collect at military posts; and they will not be supported in idleness either there or elsewhere."

General Order Number 3, read by Major General Gordon Granger, Galveston, Texas, June 19, 1865

*J*uneteenth is a bittersweet holiday. It commemorates the day in 1865 when blacks in Texas finally learned that they were free—two and a half years after the Emancipation Proclamation and two months after the surrender of Robert E. Lee. The news was delivered in Galveston, and that is where our road trip begins, June 19, 2001, where Martin Luther King Boulevard meets the beach at the Gulf of Mexico.

For two weeks we drive eleven hundred miles up the nation's midsection, halfway to Canada, visiting eighteen more MLKs: East Texas, Louisiana, Arkansas. Over to Oklahoma and up to Kansas, where we have a date in Leavenworth with eighty-nine-year-old Rosetta Stone, whose name—evoking the ancient

Michelle Coghill, doctoral candidate in anthropology, on Juneteenth in Galveston, Texas, where the holiday originated

"Old Sparky," the electric chair that took the lives of 361 prisoners between 1924 and 1964, Texas Prison Museum, Huntsville, Texas

rock whose inscription unlocked the mysteries of Egyptian hieroglyphics—leapt from a directory of the city's little Martin Luther King Drive.

There are stops that test the limits of irony: Emancipation Park along the MLK in Huntsville, Texas—prison town and execution capital of the United States. The MLK in Jasper, Texas, on which James Byrd, Jr., was walking when he climbed into a pickup truck, to be dragged to his death.

To name any street for King is to invite an accounting of how that street makes good on King's promise or mocks it. There is certainly an irony that a man viewed as an apostle of integration should have given his name to a vast network of streets that define the contours of a black nation still so separate.

But you can't live on irony, and the people we meet on these MLKs don't. They struggle in a world that exists every day in a Juneteenth twilight, straining to make real that late word of freedom.

Galveston, Texas

Craig Bowie ran two parades through Galveston this Juneteenth. His first marched in the oppressive midday heat across Martin Luther King Boulevard. The second, in the blessed relief of evening, came striding down MLK to the gulf. It was led by a funky, second-line funeral band with a saxophone, sousaphone, snare drum, and fat man with shiny black shoes and an umbrella.

The early parade has become tradition. Bowie added the second to draw folks down to the beach for his first-ever Juneteenth fireworks, another of his efforts to rouse Galveston to what he can only imagine must have been the jubilation of that original emancipation day. "They say on Juneteenth, they danced in the street," he says.

With the last liberating starburst of fireworks, Bowie, lean and boyish,

Juneteenth fireworks, where MLK hits the beach in Galveston, Texas

Strutting his stuff. Robert Stevens of the Sunrise Brass Band leads the Juneteenth Parade, Galveston, Texas.

jumps back on his heels, rears his head, and exhales whispered affirmations of joy, thanks, and relief.

But by the next morning, he is back to worrying. "I try to stay focused on the concept, the purpose, on spreading the word," he says of Juneteenth. "The deficit that I've seen is the children don't know what it really is, they don't know it's about freedom, they don't even know they're free. Man, some of them, this is all they've seen. They are so small and they see all this junk around here and they ain't never been across the causeway so they just think this is the world, and this island don't have to be like this. Not this island, not this island."

And so here, in one of the poorest corners of America, Bowie has created a shimmering, shoestring oasis, laying claim to space with the bright colors and black themes of his joyful, expressive folk art. In his big, bare-bones storefront his wife, Hope, sells shoes, his daughter, Ebony, sells Sno-Kones, and he runs what amounts to one-room schools of entrepreneurship and performing arts,

'Hood hero Craig Bowie, organizer of Juneteenth parades and fireworks, Galveston, Texas

both named for Howard "Stretch" Johnson, a tap-dancing Communist who during a brief sojourn in Galveston became Bowie's mentor.

Johnson, a Buffalo Soldier in World War II, was a Harlem blend of raconteur and activist. He performed with Duke Ellington at the Cotton Club and the Apollo Theater on 125th Street, which is now also known as MLK Boulevard. He leafleted outside Yankee Stadium in favor of integrating baseball. Before Galveston, he lived in Hawaii, where he played a lead role in establishing a state Martin Luther King holiday. He died at age eighty-five in 2000.

"Stretch was a radical," says Bowie. "He taught me how to lead."

Johnson was also, like Bowie, a recovering alcoholic. Painted on one wall of Bowie's store-school are some of the promises from the *Big Book of Alcoholics Anonymous*: "That feeling of uselessness and self-pity will disappear."

On the perpendicular wall are entrepreneurial aphorisms, borrowed from the National Foundation for Teaching Entrepreneurship, a New York–based organization that provides the curriculum for Bowie's effort to teach business skills. Things like "Think before you make a decision" and "Consider closely cost-benefit analysis and opportunity costs."

"So many things are a mental state of mind," says Bowie. "I can't figure out, man, how come, there were so many more slaves than slave owners, how come they just didn't up on them and take over."

Not many years ago, Bowie was collecting garbage in Galveston. Before that he did five years in prison, mostly in Huntsville. Before that, at twenty-five, he was shot in the face with a twelve-gauge double-barreled shotgun. A girlfriend. He lost his left eye. "In sixty days I went through being shot, my mama dead, and locked up," says Bowie.

"I ain't always lived like this," he goes on.

Shhh . . . choir practice. Robin Rhone at Shiloh AME Church, Galveston, Texas

On these streets, Bowie's history of tough times is both his credential and his inspiration.

"I want to create a miracle," he says.

Houston

The weekly Black Reality Class at the Shrine of the Black Madonna Book Store and Cultural Center on MLK Boulevard is canceled, but the writer Walter Mosley will be reading the next night, so we stay an extra day.

The Shrine and the Pan-African Orthodox Christian Church next door were founded in Detroit by the late Albert B. Cleage, Jr., who later changed his

Anika Sala, manager of the Shrine of the Black Madonna Book Store and Cultural Center, in the adjoining Pan-African Orthodox Christian Church of which the shrine is a part, Martin Luther King Boulevard, Houston

name to Jaramogi Abebe Agyeman. In its theology, as in the large mural behind the altar in the majestic church, Jesus is a young black freedom fighter.

The shrine's address may be MLK, but the spirit is much more Malcolm X. As Cleage wrote in 1972, "Dr. King's entire approach was a mystical kind of idealism which had no roots in objective reality."

Mosley appears in a large chapel just steps down from the bookstore, next to the shrine's Black Holocaust Museum. Sitting in front of a huge portrait of Malcolm X, before a rapt audience of about a hundred, Mosley quotes Malcolm telling a Harlem audience, "You have been bamboozled" by America. Blacks are not the only ones bamboozled, he says—just the most aware of it. "Black history is the only real history people should be studying in school because that's how we can learn how to overcome oppression," he says.

Sunset basketball at Sims Bayou Park, Houston, Texas

Huntsville, Texas

They celebrate Juneteenth in Huntsville at Emancipation Park on the shady Martin Luther King Boulevard. The park was founded by ex-slaves. Across the street, two sisters and a brother, all near eighty, are taking in the still of the afternoon. No, says Alberta Ferguson, they were not here for that original Juneteenth. They are the last three of nineteen children of Jack English, a railroad man who died in 1976 at the age of 110. He was born Christmas 1865. If their grandmother danced on that first Juneteenth, their father rocked in her womb.

Next door is St. Luke United CME Church. Ferguson's son-in-law, Obie Roland, used to pastor that church, until in the words of Florine Woods, he "went Baptist," and left with most of the parishioners to start a new church just through a clearing off King.

Walter Mosley before a reading at Shrine of the Black Madonna Book Store and Cultural Center, Houston

Abd' Allah Muhammad-Bey at the mosque he founded near the Texas death chamber

Woods, seventy-three, stuck with St. Luke and is now president of the usher board. Short and sweet, she has a bullet shell from an AR-15 military assault rifle on her key chain. It was a going-away gift when she retired at sixty-two after ten years as a prison guard in the picket tower at the Ellis Unit, a few miles out of town. For eight hours a shift she had to watch out over the prison yard. "You got to be standing when you eat, you can't get so relaxed." There was a toilet in the guard tower with a window and curtain to peek through. She had three weapons—the AR-15 for shooting at a distance, the twelve-gauge shotgun for up close, and the .357 Magnum for in between. She never fired a shot. Sometimes inmates in the yard would signal her to look alert, the warden was coming.

"I miss it," she says.

Next door to the church, a group of black boys, skittering around the neigh-

David Richardson and friends, Martin Luther King Drive, Huntsville, Texas

borhood on foot and bikes, collect under the Martin Luther King street sign. They are next to the low-slung public housing development on King, and they spit out the names they call it—the projects, the 'jects, the p.j.'s, the bricks.

Abd' Allah Muhammad-Bey lives there. Muhammad-Bey doesn't miss his days as a prison guard back in Wilmington, Delaware. He knows the ins and outs of imprisonment. By the time he was eleven he was in a juvenile facility in Wilmington. He was released into the custody of the Black Man's Development Center of the Moorish Science Temple, a forerunner of the Nation of Islam in seeking to connect black Americans to Muslim roots and to one another in black nationalist solidarity. He served time more recently, a few years ago, in the county jail in Houston when his now ex-wife was busted for crack. He was driving the car.

Muhammad-Bey's small apartment, like his life, is cluttered with earnest purpose. Studying toward his master's degree in family and marriage counseling at Sam Houston State University, he is already working as the first Muslim substance abuse counselor in the Texas prison system, and is developing a "whole-way house" for released inmates. Earlier in 2001 he persuaded his fellow student senators to support a death penalty moratorium, this on a campus dominated by criminal justice majors in a city dedicated like no other to executing capital offenders.

From his Moorish Science beginnings, Muhammad-Bey has come to embrace a nonracialized Orthodox Islam, "like Malcolm X," he says. He is the imam of a mosque he started in a tiny geodesic dome next to a locksmith's shop in the shadow of the death chamber. On their release, some Muslim inmates come to pray there before leaving Huntsville.

Like Craig Bowie, Muhammad-Bey seems unhardened by hard times. Like Bowie, he is on a mission to liberate black minds. "Most people here got a slave mentality," he says.

Jasper, Texas

The sky is a rich blue swept with creamy clouds, the countryside a lush green, the day warm and bright, but the simple sign, JASPER POP. 7160, sends a cold shiver down the spine.

Jasper city limits, Martin Luther King Boulevard, Jasper, Texas

Almost precisely three years earlier, many hundreds of people were lined up along Martin Luther King Boulevard for James Byrd's funeral; Greater New Bethel Baptist Church, home church to Byrd's mother and father, was filled to overflowing. The whole world was watching.

"Jesse [Jackson] wanted to preach. I told him, 'No, I'll preach,' " recalls the Reverend Kenneth O. Lyons, the pastor of New Bethel and a master of the hypnotic, singsongy preaching style that reaches far into the black past.

Lyons has deep roots hereabouts. His great-great-great-great-grandfather was Richard Seale, who as a slave founded Dixie Baptist Church—the mother church to Greater New Bethel—on a plantation seven miles outside Jasper. Seale had been brought to Jasper by his master about 1850, but according to a history written by a descendant of that master, "he first opened his eyes in the slave pens of Alexandria, Virginia," apparently in 1798, "his mother, a Negro, . . . had been captured in Africa as a child."

Sunday services at Greater New Bethel Baptist Church, Jasper, Texas

The history goes on to describe the day when the sickly infant Richard was crying loudly in his mother's arms as a parade was about to pass. "His mother tried to hush him, but she could not. People looked around—and abruptly the crowd parted. A man on a white horse rode to her and pressed a coin in her hand. Laughing, he told her to buy the baby some chocolate, that he had a long life ahead, and should not waste childhood in tears." The man, so the story goes, was George Washington.

Lyons runs a serious church. A sign on the wall carries the adage "A child brought up in Sunday School is rarely brought up in court." The church bulletin quotes the eminent black psychiatrists James P. Comer and Alvin F. Poussaint advising parents to teach children "strategies to deal with racism and the negative feelings about being black that racism incurs." However, "it is not necessary,

Ushers Edrick Scott and Courtney Powell at Greater New Bethel Baptist Church, Jasper, Texas.

San Augustine, Texas

nor is it advisable . . . to bring up race at every turn."

People in Jasper have tried hard to bury the ugliness of Byrd's murder, even tearing down the fence that for a hundred years separated black from white in the cemetery where Byrd is buried. "I never did pay attention to that fence," says Lyons. "I don't guess it makes no difference when you're dead."

San Augustine, Texas

The MLK in San Augustine seems nothing but a residential rural road in the heart of the piney woods. Then it turns ninety degrees to the left, and the street sign indicates that this is the intersection of MLK and MLK, something we have never seen before. Remarkable. We are excited.

So is a woman watching us from her front lawn. Dressed in her Sunday best, she yells at us to get off her street and out of her neighborhood, right now.

We explain our mission. "Martin Luther King had nothing to do with two white boys," she says.

Robert Gates, Gates Barber Shop, Oklahoma City, Oklahoma

We point out the uniqueness of her intersection—MLK and MLK. She looks at us with disgust. "And that's interesting?"

As we drive away, she is writing down our license plate number.

Center, Texas

Clyde Lister has "closed the lid" on some four thousand black folks in his fifty years at Hicks Mortuary on MLK in Center. The Jesus on the

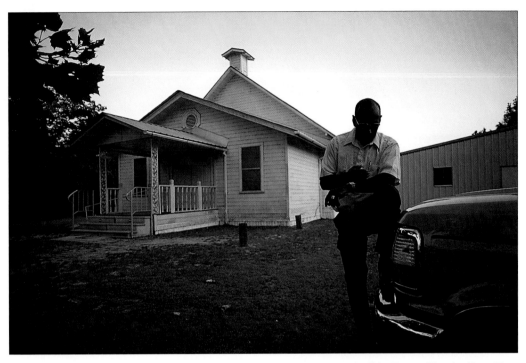

Clyde Lister at St. John Baptist Church, Africa, Texas

wall at Hicks is dark-skinned, and Hicks offers the option of placing a black rendition of the Last Supper inside the lid. We have come to Lister in hopes of gaining passage to Africa, where he lives.

Africa, Texas, is close by but along an unmarked dirt road. For about a century it has been home to twenty-some black families. The heart of Africa is the simple white St. John Baptist Church. Behind the church is a graveyard alive with fresh flowers. Lister and his good friend, Eddie Logan, a deacon of the church, figure maybe this place was named Africa because in the whippoorwill solitude a black man could imagine himself back in the homeland he had never seen.

Lister spies a cottontail hopping between headstones. "They tell me if you take a bite of rabbit and chew it up and lay it on something and come back the next morning, it's a ball of hair," he says.

Logan gives Lister a long wide-eyed stare. "Oh no," he says.

Bishop Floyd Caldwell of Greenwood Acres Full Gospel Church, Shreveport, Louisiana, with the King statue he rescued after it was rejected by residents along MLK Drive as too abstract and then placed on eBay.

"I never did try it," Lister says. "I always swallowed mine."

They burst into the loud laughter of longtime friends.

Shreveport, Louisiana

We have come to Shreveport in search of the statue of King that stood briefly at the head of Martin Luther King Drive, a major thoroughfare with an abandoned quiet to it.

The city commissioned the fifteen-hundred-pound bronze for forty thousand dollars. But the statue—in which King links supernaturally extended and contorted arms with a man and woman on either side of him—was bitterly

Eddie Logan and Clyde Lister, Africa, Texas

attacked by some who were disturbed by its abstractness. The last we had read about it, the work had been removed and put up for auction on eBay, where no one had bid more than a few thousand dollars.

But, we discover, the bronze MLK has found a good home.

"I woke up one morning and the Lord told me to call the mayor and buy the statue," says Bishop Floyd Caldwell.

Sight unseen. He paid fifteen thousand dollars raised in cooperation with a restaurateur who gave contributors catfish coupons.

At age seven, Caldwell says, he watched as his grandfather burst into his home and killed his abusive father. By 1971 Caldwell—junkie, drug dealer, pimp—was suicidal. But the night he was to do himself in, something on TV caught his attention. It was a Billy Graham Crusade. Caldwell got religion and now has two churches with among the largest congregations in Shreveport and a worldwide radio ministry.

The King statue stands in a garden between Caldwell's Greenwood Acres Full Gospel Church and the church's Family Life Center, the latter with state-of-the-art health club, bowling alley, gleaming basketball courts, elegant restaurant, witty Afrocentric reworkings of classic paintings, boardroom and offices in elegant ash wood. It all stands in jaw-dropping contrast to the often low-rent accoutrements of civic life in black America.

As Caldwell walks outside the church, children call his name and come to touch him. He says that what black folks want and need is "money and lots of it.

"The white man knows he owes us reparations. He'll never give it to us because he's mad. The white man is mad because Negroes are no longer slaves, and the Negroes are mad because the white man once had them as slaves."

Instead, he says, "the aim in America is to give every young black a felony."

On the MLK near where the King statue used to be there is a Southern University campus. There, Professor Willie Burton has compiled a remarkable archive of the city's black history. For several years he produced a calendar dense with black history for every day of the year, illustrated each month with images that provide insights into the white psyche, chilling in their banality.

For August 2000 it is a page entitled "The Ugly Face of Jim Crow" and including a reproduction of a real estate advertisement that appeared on the cover of the 1911 Shreveport City Directory. It reads: "Queensborough. The prettiest section of Shreveport for a home. We will build you a home and let you pay it out like rent. And remember you will never have a Negro for a neighbor."

Today, Queensborough is mostly black.

Texarkana

The midday sun beats hard on Martin Luther King Boulevard, a main drag across the state line with not a single pedestrian in sight. Last May, in the "cheers and jeers" column in the *Texarkana Gazette*, a reader wrote, "Naming a boulevard after James Earl Ray is a bit too much. It makes about as much sense as naming one after Martin Luther King."

Idabel, Oklahoma

"You're not a local yokel, are you?" Raeshanda Andrews asks as we purchase four newspapers from her at the E-Z Mart.

As we explain what brought us here, her eyes light up. "You're taking the trip I want to take," she says. "I was talking with a friend about this last night. Why is it always in the 'hood? Martin Luther King is always in the ghetto.

"Everything he stood for is supposed to be great for my people, and you name a street for him and it goes straight to hell," says Andrews, who was born in the housing project on what is now Idabel's MLK.

The 'hood? The ghetto? Hell? Across MLK from her projects, three horses graze lazily on sixty acres of green pasture. The horses belong to Andrew Young, a thirty-five-year-old of grace and quiet power, who hays the MLK acreage. He has a steer ranch nearby. A white doctor who took a liking to him helped him get this land, learn to work it, and sell his first hay.

Young is also the county's first and only black firefighter.

"It's all pretty cool, man," he says. "I always wanted to be a firefighter, and I always wanted to be a rancher. I'm doing just what I wanted to do."

Andrew Young—rancher, firefighter—Idabel, Oklahoma

For four hours in the slow fade of a luminous day, arrayed around the back of his pickup as the horses amble by for affection, we talk with Young and his brother Craig about life and fate and Idabel.

In 1980, Henry Lee Johnson, a fifteen-year-old black youth, was shot to death in the parking lot of the Black Hat Club, a white nightclub across a fence from the mostly black projects. Young says that Johnson—"He was like a best friend to me"—was left hanging on that fence, as in a lynching.

It's the story that spread through the black community, says Maxine Moss, Raeshanda Andrews's mother, who was living in the projects then, pregnant with Raeshanda. But Moss says Johnson actually was left lying where he was shot, where her brother found him.

Either way, by afternoon, a crowd of a hundred blacks converged on the police station demanding justice, and by night, Idabel was engulfed in violence. The Black Hat burned, and when firefighters arrived, they were shot at. A gun battle at a gas station left a white auxiliary police officer and a black man dead. The newspapers called it a race riot, but to Moss, a staff sergeant with the airforce reserve and now a civilian employee at Scott Air Force Base in Belleville, Illinois, "It was more like a black revolt."

Idabel, she says, is "one of those places, you get out of, you don't look back."

Oklahoma City, Oklahoma

The men at the very mellow Zodiac Motorcycle Club on King (every member has his own key) say that we need to meet Clara Luper, and that she is probably just down MLK rehearsing the Miss Black Oklahoma contestants.

The pageant is being held at a threadbare motel (it soon closes for good) on

Zodiac Motorcycle Club, Oklahoma City, Oklahoma

a neon-ugly, truck-stop stretch of King. Luper, who has run the show for thirty-two years, lifts it from the shabby dust of its circumstance by sheer force of will and dignity.

In 1957 she took a group of black youngsters to Harlem to perform a play she had written, *Brother President: The Story of Martin Luther King*. For the first time, they were able to eat in the same restaurant with white people. "It gave my young people a taste of freedom," Luper says.

The summer after their return—a year and a half before the sit-ins in Greensboro, North Carolina, which history usually enshrines as the first—they began sitting in at Katz Drug Store in Oklahoma City. Theirs continued for six years until, in 1964, they prevailed. Luper has been arrested twenty-six times.

Luper is loved; Luper is feared. She can be very funny, but in repose her face relaxes into a scowl. She demands, browbeats, and inspires.

Young escort Darihawn Simpson, the great-grandson of Clara Luper, Miss Black Oklahoma Pageant, Oklahoma City

Clara Luper at the Freedom Center she founded on the MLK in Oklahoma City

She schools the beauty contestants in civil rights history the week they are with her. At breakfast two days before the pageant, she announces she will give them each an oral exam on what she taught them. "The passing grade is one hundred," she says.

She gives the young women a tour of the Freedom Center she built on King to honor the heroes—from MLK and Malcolm X to Clara Luper and Robert Gates, the barber with the shop next door—who put their lives on the line in the struggle. The center was bombed and mostly destroyed in 1968. Luper rebuilt. There is now a memorial wall at the center for the 168 people killed in the Oklahoma City bombing. "I personally knew, personally, fifty of those that were killed," says Luper.

Not far up King from the Freedom Center is the Mabel Bassett Correctional Center, a women's prison. According to a notice posted on a bulletin

board inside Mabel Bassett, the prison library is looking for three books that were borrowed and never returned. They are *Someone Like You*, a Kwanzaa romance; *Sturdy Black Bridges*, a collection of black women's writing on the trials and triumphs of black womanhood; and *White Butterfly*, one of Walter Mosley's Easy Rawlins mysteries.

Mabel Bassett is home to Raeshanda Andrews's aunt, who, Raeshanda told us, used to live on the MLK in Idabel and was arrested doing crack on the MLK in Ardmore, Oklahoma. Mabel Bassett is also home to the death row where a black woman by the name of Wanda Jean Allen lived before her execution in January 2001. Allen was sentenced to death for killing the girlfriend she met doing time in Mabel Bassett for killing her last girlfriend. Her lawyers argued, to no avail, that she was not very bright and that her original lawyer was not very good.

We meet up with the Reverend Vernon Burris, resplendent in a white suit, outside Mabel Bassett's barbed-wire fence. Burris was Allen's spiritual adviser the last ten months of her life, though by the end, he says, she was the one keeping his spirits up.

Burris has all-purpose flash, which enabled him to do quite well for the many years he lived in the fleshpot of Los Angeles, first as a pimp, then turning fifty dollars into a million in real estate, and for the last sixteen years saving souls. Ten years ago he returned to Oklahoma with his own church and radio ministry. Allen's aunt, a listener, called and asked if he would go see her.

After a few months of Saturday visits, Wanda Jean Allen asked Burris to baptize her in the prison chapel's waters. On the appointed day, she brought along the other two women on death row—both white—and Burris baptized them as well.

When Allen's time came to die, she asked Burris to bear witness. "They asked if she had any last words, and she quoted a scripture that was used two thousand years ago when Christ was on the cross, when he was about to be exe-

The Reverend Vernon Burris in front of Mabel Bassett Correctional Center, where he ministered to Wanda Jean Allen in the months before her execution

Tiffany Fitzgerald at Salon 2000, Oklahoma City

cuted," he says. "She said, 'Lord forgive them, for they know not what they do.'"

Right next door to the women's prison, standing on the green lawn in front of her family's home and hair salon, Tiffany Fitzgerald is the embodiment of freedom. She is wearing a sleeveless wraparound dress with bright images of tropical vegetation, bearing on her breastbone a butterfly tattoo. Her stance and attitude perfectly express her succinct ambition, "to get away from here." She says she plans to enlist in the military. When we check back in the fall, after September 11, her mother informs us that she has decided to enroll in college instead.

Leavenworth, Kansas

Leavenworth is home to a magnificent monument to the Buffalo Soldiers, the two black cavalry units that were organized here in 1866 and were not disbanded until 1952. The monument was the brainchild of Colin Powell, when he was assigned to Fort Leavenworth. In 1992 Powell, then chairman of the Joint Chiefs of Staff, returned to dedicate the dramatic bronze of a Buffalo Soldier on horseback.

There is also a black soldier, Dwight Loving, on death row at Fort Leavenworth. Convicted of killing two white taxi drivers at Fort Hood, Texas, in 1988, Loving would be the first soldier executed since 1961. Of the twelve soldiers executed between 1954 and 1961, all but one were black.

All that's on the Martin Luther King Drive in Leavenworth is a labyrinthine

Memorial to the Buffalo Soldiers, Leavenworth, Kansas

Rosetta Stone, eighty-nine, Leavenworth, Kansas

complex of garden apartments built by two local churches. Weeks before embarking on our Juneteenth journey, we examined a reverse directory listing the names of all those residing on Leavenworth's MLK. The moment we came across the name Rosetta Stone, we knew we had found our journey's ultimate destination, and called her to describe our mission and invite ourselves over. She demurred, but we said we would call again, and when we phoned from the road and explained that we were driving 302 miles from Oklahoma City expressly to meet her, she acquiesced. When we arrive, she and Ragamuffin, her beautifully tarnished saxophone, are ready and waiting.

Rosetta Stone is her married name. She picked up the saxophone in her sixties, after her husband died. Took one lesson, but when she found out her teacher was also taking lessons, she figured, How much could he know?

Instead, she prayed on it. "God taught me how to put the notes together to play a song. I wouldn't know A-flat if I saw it walking down the street," she says.

She adjusts the mouthpiece on Ragamuffin and begins to play her version of "Jesus Never Fails." She says her air isn't what it used to be, but the tone is rich, clear, smooth.

She mostly plays in her Pentecostal church. But she also plays for herself. "If I don't encourage nobody else, I can encourage myself," she says. "I know how people feel when they're singing the blues."

Chapter 8

The Edge

They want the black neighborhoods but not the black neighbors? It's like, what are they trying to say?

Paradise Freejahlove, a.k.a. Richard Moore,
"I Love Everything About You but You"

When Johnie Wright arrived in Oakland, California, from Shreveport, Louisiana, in 1943, there were almost no black folks and no black-eyed peas. "Black-eyed peas, purple-hulled peas, buffalo fish, catfish, perch, collard greens, turnip greens. None of that stuff was here," says Wright, the Watermelon King of Oakland's Martin Luther King Way. "We brought all that here."

By the late 1960s, there were few places with a more secure spot on the map of black America than Oakland. It was hometown to the Black Panthers. (They too were sons of the South. Eldridge Cleaver was born in Wabbaseka, Arkansas. Bobby Seale was a native of Dallas, Texas. Huey P. Newton, a child of Monroe, Louisiana, was named for Huey P. Long. The Black Panther name and logo were born in the Black Belt of Alabama.)

But Oakland has been getting less black—more polyglot—for twenty years. Now the old Panther headquarters on MLK is the It's All Good Bakery, a stop on a Black Panther Legacy Tour. In his neighborhood, Wright says, with every house sold, the seller is black and the buyer is not. Black people are moving east,

Johnie Wright, the Watermelon King of MLK Way, Oakland, California

into what is known as the California Delta. "It's another migration," says Wright.

The same year that Wright arrived in Oakland, up the West Coast black folks arriving in Portland, Oregon—drawn as they were to Oakland by the lure of jobs in wartime shipbuilding—encountered signs in store windows all up and down Union Avenue: WHITE TRADE ONLY. Today, Union Avenue is Martin Luther King Boulevard, the spine of the neighborhood they call "the soul of Portland."

But the ghetto in this, one of America's whitest big cities, would be laughed out of any serious national competition. Too leafy. Too ruly. And these days, yesterday's ghetto is today's good investment. Property values are rising.

Sitting in Stellar Coffee, one of the rare black-owned businesses on MLK, Charles Bolden despairs of the black future on the block. "In ten years," he worries, "I don't think any blacks are going to be here."

Neighborhood mural, Oakland. Berkeley artist Edythe Boone walks past a mural whose creation she directed.

Maya Griffith at a gospel show, Miracles Club, Portland, Oregon

The history of African Americans is one of restless movement born of hope and fear. Blacks have been slaves, immigrants, pioneers, and refugees in their own land, relocating and re-creating the life of a people, claiming space and naming it. In years to come, there will be new MLK streets in the latest black communities to come of age, as surely as there will be some where the street sign Martin Luther King marks a place fading from black.

On the West Coast, in Oakland and Portland, we encounter two outposts of blackness, perched on the edge of Africa America and on the edge of change.

D'Asia Calhoun, great-granddaughter of the founders, at Marcus Books in Oakland

We are on MLK Way in Oakland on May 19, 2001, Malcolm X's birthday. He would have been seventy-six. At Marcus Books, directly across from the Watermelon King, Blanche Richardson is playing a tape of Malcolm X delivering his speech "The Ballot or the Bullet." Her father, Julian, who died in 2000, loved Malcolm, committing his words to memory. The MLK mural painted on the front of the store is inscribed with a quotation from King's "Letter from a Birmingham Jail" that would have met Malcolm's muster: "Freedom is never voluntarily given by the oppressor. It must be demanded by the oppressed."

The store is named for Marcus Garvey, the father of modern black nationalism. Julian Richardson grew up in Birmingham, Alabama, the son of a Garveyite. He met his wife, Raye, at Tuskegee University. Together they founded the Marcus Books stores in San Francisco in 1960 and in Oakland in 1976. They were married fifty-eight years and, their daughter says, "in love the entire time."

When Blanche was growing up, her father would ask her and her siblings every single day, "What have you done for your people today?" And, she says, "You better have an answer." She spent much of her youth picketing for her people, sometimes with only other members of her family joining her on the line.

Her mother, who was the head of the Black Studies Department at San Francisco State, still writes a column—called "Hi Babe," for her signature greeting—in *The Sun-Reporter*, a black newspaper. "She doesn't play," says Blanche. A recent column begins, "There are many white men who would joyfully buy a one-way ticket to Hell if guaranteed that a black man would be forced to carry their baggage."

Every morning, Blanche Richardson leaves the home she shares with her mother above the Marcus Books her sister manages in San Francisco and drives to the Marcus Books that she manages in Oakland. She rarely strays far from the store. It would be a terribly cloistered existence were it not for the fact that the world, the black world, comes to her. Virtually every black poet, novelist, self-help guru, great thinker, would-be savior, and celebrity author comes to Marcus to read and be seen. Marcus is the heart and hearth of MLK in Oakland and the black community beyond, crackling, inviting.

On a slow Sunday, those wandering through Marcus include a purposeful librarian who orders books for a nearby school system, the Jamaican dub poet Mutabaruka, and the Howertons, Joseph and Elsie, an antique and exquisitely appointed couple who drop by every Sunday to pick up three copies each of *The Sun-Reporter* and *The Final Call* and to report themselves, in Joseph's fixed phrase, "just this side of marvelous."

Richardson is warm and wry. She made a deal with Johnie Wright. Every student who spends more than fifty dollars on books gets a free watermelon. "That way they wouldn't starve buying textbooks."

She has also just edited the book *Best Black Women's Erotica*, including contributions from herself and her daughter, who also works in the store and is now pregnant with her second child.

"If they ever clone you, I want one," Richardson says, suppressing a small smile, as she introduces the writer Kevin Powell, who appears at Marcus the

Poet AfroKen (Ken Marcelous), emcee, at Tongue Tuesday, Eli's Mile High Club, Oakland

night of Malcolm X's birthday. Born between the assassinations of Malcolm and Martin, Powell is here to talk about his new book, *Step into a World,* a collection of writings of people of his generation.

His audience includes the hip-hop journalists Davey D, who has a show on KPFA just up MLK in Berkeley, and Allen Gordon, the former editor of the defunct magazine *Rap Pages,* now working at a record store in Berkeley, who gets a big hug from Richardson. He introduces her to his mother.

"I feel hip-hop has got to be documented, and we've got to do it," says Powell. "I don't want to see *Ken Burns's Hip-Hop.*

"The beautiful thing to me about the hip-hop generation—we really don't give a damn what white folks think about us," says Powell. "We really don't."

Head north from Marcus, and MLK Way (sometimes called Milky Way) coasts into the retro cool of Berkeley. This being Malcolm X Day, the very integrated Berkeley High School on MLK is closed, though there are some students in the park next door raising money for their class trip to Cuba. The school's jazz ensemble plays the Montreux Jazz Festival.

Head south a few blocks from Marcus and you are at Eli's Mile High Club, "home of the West Coast blues." Tonight a rhythm and blues band fronted by a Japanese guitarist plays Wilson Pickett. A black couple in cowboy outfits two-steps. Two young men in matching English boarding school suits and haircuts dance in affectionate embrace.

We return to Eli's for their weekly poetry slam, hosted by the poet AfroKen, otherwise known as Ken Marcelous, who lives on MLK in Berkeley.

The poet and arts activist Paradise Freejahlove, a.k.a. Richard Moore, who has mapped "the Great Pyramid of Little Nubia," a triangular black business district in Oakland and Berkeley bisected by MLK Way, is performing his piece "I Love Everything About You but You," singing it in his rich baritone to a jazz accompaniment.

"They want the black spirit. They want the black mind. They want the black soul. They want the black behind," it goes, then repeats each time the refrain, "They want the black," with a litany of the desired—muscle, heart, music, art, rhythm, hips, power, lips, style, talk, skill, walk, rod, heat, coffee, meat, land, gold, diamonds, coal, oil, race, earth, space, dollar, gods.

"They want the black everything but me and you, now that's odd. They want the black neighborhoods but not the black neighbors? It's like, what are they trying to say?"

Sunday morning we arrive bright and early at the storefront Apostolic Church of Deliverance Jesus Name Temple, a block up MLK from Marcus. For five hours we are back in deepest Mississippi.

Elder Willie Kelly, out of Edwards, Mississippi, leads the singing of "Jesus on the Main Line" and "Jesus Is Real to Me." "I used to live in the middle of a cotton field," he says.

Lillie Luckett, the rock of her church, picked cotton on Delta land tended by the grandfather of the murdered Emmett Till. When she saw the famous

Lillie Luckett, Apostolic Church of Deliverance Jesus Name Temple, Oakland

photo in *Jet* magazine of the tortured Till in his open coffin she remembers
thinking, "That family always had trouble."

Luckett is Sister Luckett. She is Mother Luckett. She has suffered with
rheumatoid arthritis, cancer, and congestive heart failure, yet she goes on. Church
supper every Sunday. The food bank every third Saturday. She has a community
garden near her sky blue house. Her husband, Hillary Luckett—Lucky—owns
the car wash the other side of Marcus Books, where he sits for hours in a large
caged area peering out at life on MLK from behind dark Mississippi-bluesman
sunglasses.

For years Lillie Luckett has been on the committee that meets at Marcus
and plots ways to bring back the bustle—still keen in memory—to long, fallow
stretches of MLK. "Everything falls on my shoulders," she says.

Her pastor, Bishop Robert T. McGee, now in his eighties and disappearing into his burgundy double-breasted suit, has his own apocalyptic vision of what needs to happen. "We need to tear everything down here," he says. "Everything goes. I'm tired of this old stuff."

Luckett says she thinks we should meet with some people in the neighborhood about the future of MLK Way while we are in town.

The following day we are in Marcus Books when we notice a neat stack of nicely produced leaflets next to the cash register announcing an "important community meeting" at Luckett's church. We are the featured attraction.

We do not prove to be a big draw. In addition to the Lucketts, the bishop, and Elder Kelly, two other people show up—an older black woman and a young white woman, just moved into the neighborhood.

The Watermelon King's artless stand looks like it could have been relocated direct from the MLK in Shreveport. But his business card, made at the Marcus print shop behind the bookstore, is a little Bay Area work of art—his name and title superimposed over an exhaustive accounting of his inventory ("peanuts, pecans, black eye peas, butter beans, yams, cream peas, speckled butter beans . . .").

A slightly heavyset black man approaches. "Where are your salted peanuts?" he asks. "We don't carry no salted peanuts," says Wright, training his chalk blue eyes on the customer. "Too many Negroes have high blood pressure."

A deaf woman stops by and writes Wright a note. He writes back.

"She ain't no customer," he says after she leaves. "She likes to talk, to write, to tell me about her life. I listen. I'm a good listener."

Johnie's wife, Mildred, is ready for the Watermelon King to end his reign. He says that when the right offer for his property comes his way, he'll take it. But he is in no hurry, so Mildred Wright comes to the stand each day and sits by his side.

They met in 1961, when she came to Oakland from Hempstead, Texas, to stay with her uncle, a friend of Johnie's. "At the time," she says, "I was twenty-one, he was thirty-seven. The first thing he said to me was, 'Turn around, let me look at you,' and I said, 'I'm not,' and my aunt said, 'Turn around and let him look at you.' When I turned around he said, 'I'm going to marry you,' and I said, 'No, you're not.'

"We've been married thirty-four years, we've been together thirty-nine years," she says. "It's been a good life together. We did good."

They have a daughter who lives with them along with her two boys, eleven and fifteen. "My grandkids get out of school, they come here," says Johnie Wright. "They are the right age to get in trouble."

Octavius Miller remembers coming off the Greyhound bus in Oakland when he moved from Flint, Michigan, in 1979. He was twelve. "It was scary and exciting at the same time. I had never seen that many black people in my whole life."

He met the Black Panthers founder Huey Newton—"He told me I could be anything I wanted to be"—and sold the Panther newspaper on the street.

But within a few years, the Oakland streets had turned mean and Miller's life had become a procession of funerals. In 1993 he escaped to Portland, and it is on the Martin Luther King Boulevard there that we meet him. He is on the balcony of Yam Yam's Southern Barbecue. The owner, Larry Matthews, who was known back in his hometown of Birmingham, Alabama, as Sweet Daddy Yam Yam, is serving ribs to Miller and about twenty young black men associated with RBL (Ruthless by Law) Posse, a popular Bay Area rap group that Miller is promoting in Portland. (With his brother, Miller also owns a record store on the MLK in Tacoma, Washington.)

RBL promises a show of "hard, rugged, dangerous music."

"Where am I going to? Where am I headed? I'm joyriding with the paramedics. I'm gassed off anesthetics. Our whole life seems pathetic. Forget it. There ain't no Mister Rogers on my block. Just the neighborhood thugs with their nine cocked."

On New Year's Day 1996, RBL's Mr. Cee—Hubert "Kyle" Church III—was killed. He was twenty-two, shot nine times near the San Francisco projects where he grew up. Seven months later Miller's younger brother, the gifted rapper Seagram, was killed in a barrage of bullets in Oakland. His posthumous release, *Soul on Ice*, included the cut "Sleepin' in My Nikes." "Every day and night. Livin' in the life. They got me sleepin' in my Nikes. It's do or die against my rivals. I could give a [****] 'cause it's all about survival."

One of the RBL crew recognizes us from the MLK in Oakland. He does auto detailing in the lot behind Luckett's car wash. The elaborately painted RBL van had been parked in the street between Luckett's and Marcus Books all week. We agree that Mr. Luckett is as ornery as Mrs. Luckett is kind.

RBL has a new CD, *Hostile Takeover*, and is appearing that night at Portland's House of Grooves. The show is throbbing, packed with young people black and white. "The black experience is really interesting now," says Miller. "As much as white America hates black America—of course not all, but most of it—still we're the trendsetters. We're still surviving and they're still wondering how we're surviving."

RBL Posse at House of Grooves, Portland

NASCAR event at the Portland Speedway

Miller likes living in Portland but says you have to be very secure in your blackness. "It's a subliminal ghetto," he says. "In Portland, you're surrounded by whiteness."

Head north on MLK, and it disappears into Interstate 5 just past the trailer park and the Portland Speedway.

At the Friday night NASCAR event at the speedway, there are very few black people. We are surprised to come upon some white people handing out NAACP leaflets. On closer inspection, it is not NAACP but NCAAP—the National Coalition Against Autopsy Photos—concerned with Dale Earnhardt's posthumous privacy.

Racial change is evident and imminent along Portland's MLK. Miller says space on the boulevard that cost $10,000 in 1993 would now go for $150,000 to $200,000. We hear the same from others.

The local weekly paper lists a nightclub named 6616 Martin Luther King Boulevard. When we arrive, we find it is actually a house awaiting demolition that a young drummer and vocalist named Melanie Goldberg has transformed into a place where bands can play and friends can come hear them. It's cleverly decorated with the cartoon sophistication of *Pee-Wee's Playhouse*.

On a weekday night more than sixty white twenty-somethings—in a mix of glam, goth, and grunge styles—are partying to the live, screaming, cabaret punk of Get Hustle and its tattooed diva, Valentine.

After commenting on the "eye candy" that attracts him to 6616, Joel Hanson, a student of urban planning and community development, explains that young white people would not have come to something like this on MLK a few years ago. "There used to be gunshots, it was like really pretty gnarly," he says. But the police relocated a substation onto MLK, and people have started investing money. The tone of the street has changed. "People call this the ghetto still," says Hanson, "but that's a joke."

To Charles Bolden this is all pretty simple. Whites want to reclaim the "reserve" where black folks have been living.

6616 Martin Luther King Boulevard, Portland

We meet Bolden at Stellar, an upscale coffee shop on MLK owned and run by his friends Ronald Taylor and Taylor's wife, Edwina Wasson. Stellar was one of a half-dozen black cafés written up in the December 2000 issue of *Black Enterprise* magazine. It's making money, but it was a struggle getting the original financing, and Taylor and Wasson lost their home getting Stellar off the ground.

Bolden is a truck driver, his first name written in blue-collar script on his work shirt. But he is really a scholar, student, and bard of the black experience. Lean, athletic, and eloquent, he can rhapsodize about the recording date and personnel of a favorite Miles Davis session, or recount with fresh outrage the details of the police killing of the Chicago Black Panthers Fred Hampton and Mark Clark in the predawn of December 4, 1969.

He grew up in New York. When he was ten, his nineteen-year-old brother took him to hear Malcolm X speak in Tompkins Park in Brooklyn. Five and a half hours in the brilliant sun, he recalls, and "nothing but beauty."

Bolden comes to Stellar mostly to "soul talk" with Taylor as day tapers into night. He frets about the future on MLK because he does not believe that black folks in Portland will defend their turf. "Back East it's different," he says.

Eight years Bolden has driven his 1993 Mustang the three thousand miles from the MLK in Portland to the MLK, 125th Street, in Harlem—ten hours a stint, three and a half days, twelve tanks of gas—to spend a couple of weeks being renewed in blackness. "It's just the people, the refreshing orientation again of being home and talking with people about deep subjects on the subway where you miss your stop you're so engrossed in the topic and a guy will tell you, so-and-so is going to be at CCNY, Angela's in town, Odetta is going to be performing over there," he says. "It's like the drums. You go home and you start listening to the drums. Here there's no drums beating."

But that doesn't mean folks aren't listening for them, at Yam Yam's, at *The Portland Observer*, the black paper on King, and at Stellar, where for hours on end Taylor and Bolden and Dionne Peeples, the former journalist who, as a public relations consultant, conceived the neighborhood catchphrase "soul of Portland," welcome our stories about Lester Finney in Belle Glade, Tumbleweed in Selma, or Rose Marie Black and Stoney Burke in Chicago, like news from home.

At Stellar we also meet Michael Barber, just relocated by his computer sales company from his hometown of Memphis, Tennessee, and living in a Portland suburb. He is drawn to MLK to find a church, to find guys to play ball with, to get his hair cut at Geneva's Shear Perfection, a big barber and beauty shop.

On Saturday morning, the men and women cutting hair at Geneva's banter across the room, and Portland radiates a small-town glow in the warmth of their gossip, jokes, and teasing. Recapping Friday night, the barber Paul Knauls, Jr., (his family owns the place) muses, "It now takes us all night long to do what we used to do all night long."

That afternoon there is a gospel show a few blocks down King at the Miracles Club, home to a dozen twelve-step programs. Onstage, young black women

Dionne Peeples, Portland

Dee Dee Jack at a gospel show, Miracles Club, Portland

in whiteface and black body stockings offer an emotive ballet to the song "We Fall Down but We Get Up."

At midnight we're at KBOO, the public radio station, with Octavius Miller. "What's up, Portland? Octavius in the midnight hour. You know how we do it every Saturday night. You're out there partying, you're riding the strip. You know it's all good. Welcome to two hours of nonstop hip-hop. I got RBL Posse, they're going to be in the house."

Sunday morning, the tiny MLK storefront Church of the Living God Pillar and Ground of the Truth, Temple Number 3, carries us home, in this case to Waco, Texas, where Pastor Sylvester Green began preaching. It is a family operation. Green's wife runs the Sunday School, his son is the music director, and his

Paul Knauls, Jr., gives Carter Vann a haircut at Geneva's Shear Perfection, Portland

son's wife is the choir director. Besides the Greens, there are only three adults at church, and twenty-seven children.

"Where are all the parents?" the pastor asks. "For twenty-five years I grew the children, I can't do it anymore."

"Jesus is going to fix it," the children sing. "Jesus will fix it."

Sunday is also the sixth anniversary of Reflections, a black bookstore and café, diagonally across MLK from Geneva's. "We take over where the churches and beauty parlors leave off," says the co-owner O. B. Hill, whose family roots are in Birmingham, Alabama.

Yes, Hill says, Portland's MLK is changing. "If people cannot afford to stay, they leave." And, he continues, "Wherever they are moving to, you can rest assured that there are people moving out as they move in, 'cause that's the nature of this game. Once black people begin to move into a community, white people exit it.

"Movement is as natural as the movement of the sun," Hill says. "You have the most creative people on the Earth. Wherever we move, we'll be able to get by."

Rochelle Mayfield at a gospel show, Miracles Club, Portland

Mercedes Slocum and her son Marion at Geneva's Shear Perfection, Portland

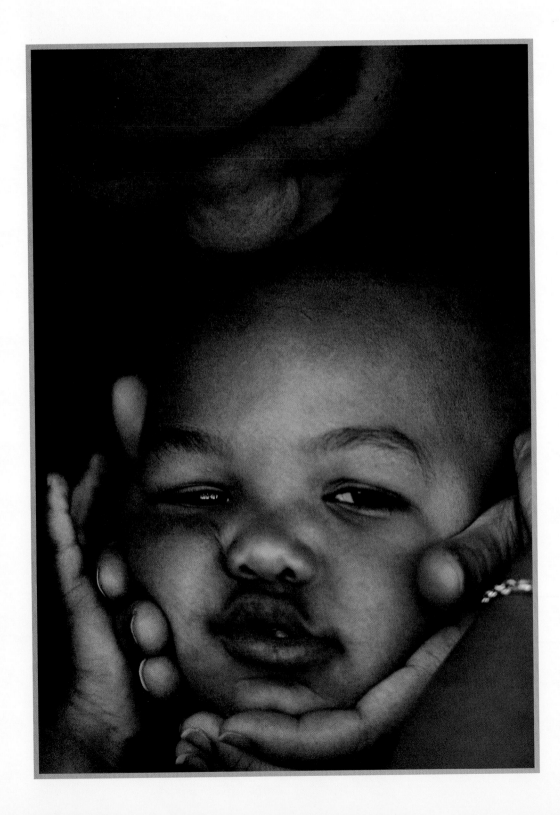

Chapter 9

The Broadway of Blackness

Face like a chocolate bar: full of nuts and sweet.

Langston Hughes, "125th Street"

Franco Gaskin—that is Franco the Great, the Picasso of Harlem—first became aware of Martin Luther King, Jr., in 1958, the same year Gaskin moved to Harlem from his native Panama. It was Sunday, September 21, and a photo of King, the picture of calm, was spread across Page One of the *Daily News*.

Gaskin was twice startled. "I was surprised to see a black man on the newspaper cover in those days. When I saw his picture, I was impressed." Then too there was the seven-inch letter opener protruding from King's chest where a forty-three-year-old black woman by the name of Izola Curry had plunged it with her paranoid declaration, "You've made enough people suffer!" King was signing copies of his first book, *Stride Toward Freedom*, at Blumstein's department store on 125th Street in Harlem, the street that now also bears King's name.

MARTIN LUTHER KING STABBED, read the *Daily News* headline, identifying

"I Had a Dream," Harlem, New York

Franco "the Great" Gaskin, the Picasso of Harlem

King as "leader of a bus boycott by Negroes in Montgomery, Ala." In the photo a small, faint circle of blood stains King's shirt around the blade, the point of which is pressed against his aorta. And, as King recalled in a speech ten years later, the last night of his life, in Memphis, "It came out in *The New York Times* the next morning that if I had merely sneezed I would have died."

From his bed in Harlem Hospital, King said he felt no ill will, only concern "that a climate of hatred and bitterness so permeates areas of our nation that inevitably deeds of extreme violence must erupt." Curry, who came out of nowhere, disappeared into the mists of history while her intended victim came to be the commanding figure of that most consequential decade to come.

Today, a quarter century since the store went out of business, the vertical BLUMSTEIN sign remains one of the most recognizable landmarks along the Harlem streetscape, but there is no plaque, no marker, nothing to indicate that

Martin Luther King nearly died here—only a mournful mural of King, a tear dripping from his eye, painted on one of the corrugated metal riot gates protecting the lobby entrance to the long-vacant upstairs floors.

"Remember," the legend under the mural reads, "I had a dream. It is for you to finish it." It is signed by the artist, Franco Gaskin—that is Franco the Great, the Picasso of Harlem.

When he first came to Harlem, Gaskin visited bars and restaurants in the neighborhood and offered to paint murals in their establishments for free to get his name and work around, but they always turned him down. He was puzzled until a friend explained: "Franco, they think you want to case the joint."

But Gaskin says that in the fearful aftermath of King's assassination, businesses along 125th replaced their old accordion gates with the more forbidding riot gates and so, in death, King provided Gaskin with his subject matter, his inspiration, and his canvas. Today the south side of 125th between Seventh and Eighth Avenues, directly across the street from the Apollo Theater, is a gallery of Gaskin's inspired riot gate murals.

"It's their business when the gates go up and mine when the gates come down," says Gaskin, except, of course, for those like the King mural that front vacant space and are there to be seen at all times. The King mural especially has become a favored photo opportunity for the busloads of tourists, many foreign, who come to Harlem, particularly on Sundays, when Gaskin is there to greet them. But curiously, he says, black folks in Harlem never mention the King mural to him, never even seem to take note of it. "It strikes me very, very, very funny," he says.

Harlem is funny that way.

It's rare that anyone calls 125th Street in Harlem Martin Luther King Boulevard. But it is. Just like Eighth Avenue is Frederick Douglass Boulevard, Seventh Avenue is Adam Clayton Powell Boulevard, and Sixth Avenue—Lenox Avenue up here—is also Malcolm X Boulevard. Harlem is like that, so chockablock with black consciousness that every intersection sounds like the title of a black studies seminar.

Crossroads

MLK—125th Street—is the single most recognized and self-aware black street in the world, the main street of Harlem, itself "a city within a city, the greatest Negro city in the world," as that Renaissance man, James Weldon Johnson, then the first black CEO of the NAACP, described it in 1925.

It is the Broadway of blackness—a bustling bazaar of street preachers, sidewalk artists, and seasoned eccentrics, of card table peddlers with books on blacks, blacks on tape, two-dollar sweaters, and soap made by "people who look just like you," of tight knots of African hair braiders, wrapped tropical bright, calling out for customers, of chicken jerked and chicken fried. Every last light pole and utility box is plastered with handbills demanding self-knowledge, freedom, action.

Want the latest analysis of how global capitalism is going to sweep blacks out of Harlem? You can buy *Harlem Ain't Nothin' but a Third World Country* right on the street, and this being 125th, you can debate the author, Mamadou

Chinyelu, because he is the card table vendor who just sold it to you. Want art so cutting edge they call it "post-black"? Check out the show at the Studio Museum in Harlem.

Harlem holds menace, as King learned. But it can also be friendly in a hustling New York kind of way, laid out low and broad like a great village with barely a tall building in sight and the best light in Manhattan.

There is history on every corner.

The day before he was stabbed at Blumstein's, King was heckled by black nationalists at a rally for school integration in front of the Hotel Theresa (everybody stayed there), now converted to office space at the corner of MLK and Adam Clayton Powell.

Six years later, in June 1964, Malcolm X telegrammed King in St. Augustine, Florida, amid violence and threats against King's life, offering to send some "brothers" to give the KKK "a taste of its own medicine"—return address, the

Street vendor, 125th Street (Martin Luther King Boulevard), Harlem

Theresa, where Malcolm's Organization of Afro-American Unity was ensconced.

At the corner of MLK and Malcolm X is the cramped Magic Johnson's Starbucks, like every other Starbucks but for its Harlem habitués. Outside, a natty black Muslim in earth brown suit and hat breaks briefly from his brisk hawking of *The Final Call* to face Mecca and say noon prayers framed in the Starbucks window. A regular, wild-eyed and lanky, who is forever bouncing a tiny little ball, enters and calls a greeting to the man who has been sitting in the far corner for hours, writing. "What's up?"

"Anything that's not down" comes the writer's reply, and then again, this time accenting the first syllable. "Anything that's not down."

We are on MLK in Harlem for Martin Luther King Day 2001. Around the corner on Madison Avenue, the redoubtable Reverend Al Sharpton draws his usual who's who of New York politics, from Hillary Clinton on down, to his annual MLK tribute at the House of Justice. That's what he calls his bare-bones ballroom just up a dark stairway from the shabby storefront below. Across town, at the Krispy Kreme at MLK and Frederick Douglass, a sign pasted on the door promises free glazed doughnuts in King's honor. And along with some special MLK church services, that's about it.

The day before, Sunday, we are upstairs from the Krispy Kreme at the mother house of the United House of Prayer for All People here in what they call Sweet Honey, Heaven Harlem. The church was founded in 1919 by a Cape Verdean immigrant, Sweet Daddy Grace, a flamboyant, faith-healing revival preacher who died in 1960 and whose successors have also been called Sweet Daddy. Today there are 132 congregations, and all the church properties are bought and paid for, says Malcolm Barksdale, a brother of the church who we meet in the House of Prayer's big cafeteria, where they serve simple soul food for next to nothing to anyone who cares to come.

The House of Prayer is a vivid church. They baptize new members using fire hoses on the streets of Harlem. But the great gift of the church can be found

A brother of the Nation of Islam selling The Final Call, *corner of Malcolm X and Martin Luther King boulevards, Harlem*

in its literal interpretation of the joyous injunction of Psalm 150. "Hallelujah," it says. "Praise him with the blast of the horn." Out of the House of Prayer comes the sacred shout-band music, a divine Dixieland that infuses their worship services. It is performed by the various churches' magnificent many-trombone brass bands, the most illustrious of which is Harlem's McCollough Sons of Thunder, led by Elder Edward Babb, lean, lissome, and very, very cool.

In 1927 James Weldon Johnson transformed into poetry seven sermons of old-time black preachers—who sometimes called themselves "sons of thunder"—in a collection entitled *God's Trombones*. The trombone, Weldon explained, is the instrument most capable of rendering all the emotions of the human voice, only louder.

On this Sunday the Sons of Thunder—nine trombones plus trumpet, tuba, cymbals, drums, and way in back an extremely old but kicking woman with a

Elder Edward Babb of McCollough Sons of Thunder, Harlem

washboard—are wailing like Heaven's house band, enveloping in their rapturous sound the twenty-thousand-square-foot sanctuary with its thirty-foot peaked ceiling.

"Sometimes you got to shake it out," declares Apostle H. M. Swaringer, the pastor. "Sometimes you got to shout it out."

When a woman rises, sways, and twitches into a fit of reverie, trilling in tongues, her church sisters in starched white uniforms coolly move in to steady and support. In pews in the rear of the sanctuary, thirty young Japanese women on a "Soul Tour" of Harlem watch in rapt stillness despite the mimed encouragement from the old lady with the washboard to rise, to writhe.

Babb's day job is driving a charter bus. He's lost other jobs—insurance salesman, hospital technician—for missing work after playing into the wee hours of the previous morning, or leaving town to play at the Clinton White House, the

Opera House in Sydney, Australia, or the world festival of sacred music in Fez, Morocco.

At the White House, where they played "We Shall Overcome," Babb says Hillary Clinton grew flushed, requesting an encore. "The doors in the White House were shaking," the First Lady said later. "The chandeliers were quaking."

Sikhulu Shange at the Record Shack, Harlem

A year and a half (and several visits to hear the Sons of Thunder at the House of Prayer) later, while visiting the MLK in Idabel, Oklahoma, we meet Virginia Hill, a retired schoolteacher who recalls her time in Harlem going to graduate school at Columbia University on Oklahoma's dime because they would not permit her to go to graduate school in Oklahoma. When we ask if she ever went to any Harlem nightclubs, she replies no, but that there was the time she went to this church to see Sweet Daddy Grace.

"He came in and people were just, you can't imagine, hugging and screaming." To get a better look at Grace being led to his throne, she climbed up on a chair. "I know you don't do that in church, but everybody else was. They had these great big tubs for money and people were throwing in bills. I don't know whether they were ones, fives, tens, or hundreds." The horns hollered. "It was a jolly jump music, I don't know, because I'm a Methodist and used to kind of quiet. I just had never seen anything like it."

"Harlem's known around the world, people want to come to see Harlem," says Sikhulu Shange. Shange has owned the Record Shack below the House of Prayer on 125th for twenty-two years but says that, like others who sustained the street during lean times, he is now "up against the wall" of gentrification.

At six foot four, a Zulu in African dress, Shange is a man of regal bearing by turns polemical and playful. His *r*'s roll elegantly off his tongue. His long, narrow store is barely wider than he is tall. He first came to New York to perform on Broadway as part of a South African theater troupe. He refused to return to apartheid.

In the worst day in recent Harlem history, a cold day in December 1996, a black street vendor walked into Freddy's, a white-owned clothing store on MLK, and shouted, "All blacks out." He set the store ablaze and opened fire, killing eight people—white, Hispanic, and black—himself included. He apparently acted in demented solidarity with ongoing protests, backed by Al Sharpton, against Freddy's, which was threatening to evict its subtenant, Shange's Record Shack. (In his book, *Al on America*, Sharpton fondly recalls buying records from Shange after James Brown concerts at the Apollo.)

Five years later Freddy's is back doing brisk business as Uptown Jeans, and Shange, now dealing directly with agents of the United House of Prayer upstairs, which owns the building, is again facing rent increases that he fears will put him out of business. Worse yet, he also now faces competition from an HMV store (HMV is the world's largest music retailer) that is so mammoth and modern it seems to exist at a far distance on the time-space continuum from the

Dance of Remembrance, Annual Tribute to Our Ancestors of the Middle Passage, Coney Island, New York

Middle Passage ceremony, Coney Island

Record Shack but, unfortunately for Shange, is in fact located right across Frederick Douglass in the Harlem USA Mall on 125th.

Six months later, on a radiant June day in 2001, we are by the beach at Coney Island for a numinous ceremony of remembrance of the black lives lost in the Middle Passage from African freedom to American bondage. We are here because Jolivette Anderson, the Poet Warrior we met nineteen months earlier on the MLK in Jackson, Mississippi, is performing. There is drumming and ethereal dancing by the lapping waters, black skin robed entirely in white.

The next day Anderson is appearing at the thirty-first annual Show and Prove gathering of the Five Percent Nation in Harlem. "I told them about you," she says. "They didn't say you couldn't come. But they didn't say you could." She suggests calling Born Justice Allah, who is handling arrangements for the Show and Prove.

The Five Percent Nation—more formally the Nation of Gods and Earths—

was founded in Harlem in 1963 by Clarence 13X, who left the Nation of Islam, changed his name to Allah, and taught that the black man is God and that 5 percent of the people know that truth. Allah rapped his liturgy in a slow, methodical cadence, emphasizing unexpected syllables in what proved to be hypnotic fashion, especially to the young people who were his target audience.

In 1965 Allah was arrested when police busted up a rally where he was speaking in front of the Theresa, and he was sent away for two years to psychiatric hospitals. But the Nation grew all the while, and on his release in 1967, Allah built a good relationship with New York Mayor John Lindsay, and the Five Percenters helped keep the peace in Harlem after King's assassination in 1968. The next year Allah himself was shot to death at the MLK Towers in Harlem. Today his teachings have gained an especially receptive audience with black men in prison and in the world of hip-hop music, where Five Percent allusions abound.

When we hear back from Born Justice Allah, the news is good. "It's not a problem for you to come to the Show and Prove," he says. "Peace."

The gathering inside the Harriet Tubman School in Harlem has drawn Five Percenters, mostly men, from across the country. We are greeted at first warily, then warmly.

To much enthusiasm, Anderson performs her piece "One World."

"On these very streets fashioned of concrete and sand, violence and disease destroy the life of the black man. Along the Nile we built on rock. In America we build on sand," she says. "From the caramel to the cream and the bronze to charcoal color scheme, we feel we can't fight the white man and win, so we fight each other and lose, again and again and again. When will it end?"

"One day," says Anderson, "black people will learn to fight the real enemy."

White family regarding Middle Passage ceremony, Coney Island

A few weeks later we are back in Harlem for a thirty-ninth-anniversary performance at the House of Prayer by the Sons of Thunder. We have flown in from Kansas City after completing our two-week Juneteenth road trip and have ended up, in a mix-up, staying in a hotel at the farthest end of Lower Manhattan from Harlem. But the moment we leave the hotel, we notice a handbill pasted to the side of a Dumpster advertising a series of events—featuring Haki Madhubuti, Walter Mosley, Amiri Baraka, and others—that night and the next day marking the seventy-fifth anniversary of the Schomburg Center for Research in Black Culture in Harlem. (When we return to the same spot fifteen minutes later, the Dumpster is gone, vanished.) We are in Harlem to hear Baraka recite "Why is we Americans? Wherever we is the same black belt. Ain't never been free since we was selt!" And later in that same poem, "Elvis king indeed. If Elvis Presley is king, who is James Brown? God?"

On July 30, 2001, Bill Clinton, who has chosen to locate his office on 125th, is formally welcomed to Harlem amid a giddy carnival of choreographed adulation and protest. "I am finally home," says the former president, who, more pink than white, now finds himself the most famous person on the most famous black street in the world. At the Record Shack, Shange can only shake his head. "The jig is up," he says.

Upstairs, in the House of Prayer cafeteria, Malcolm Barksdale, who deals in Harlem real estate and is writing a book about the neighborhood he loves, says the space is just too prime to remain forever black. "Harlem has always been owned by whites," he says, and the former president's coming is only boosting already booming property values. "I'm happy Clinton is here."

Jolivette Anderson, the Poet Warrior, waiting to perform at the annual Show and Prove, Five Percent Nation, Harlem

Gentrification can manifest itself in unlikely ways. On a subway approaching the 125th Street station, a young white man, looking fit and preppy, steps to the center of the car, cradling a small wicker basket. "I am trying to keep my apartment. I am going to sing," he says. He draws a deep breath, closes his eyes, and launches into a tenor rendition of Stevie Wonder's "Higher Ground": "People keep on learnin'. Soldiers keep on warrin'. World keep on turnin'. 'Cause it won't be too long."

We return to Harlem the Thanksgiving after September 11.

At the House of Prayer, Elder Babb says that fifty members of the church worked at the World Trade Center but not one life among them was lost. Engine 36 on MLK in East Harlem also did not lose anyone. The firehouse is covered in colorful cards of thanks, and passing schoolchildren swarm around the firefighters seeking autographs. At the military recruiting station on King, Sergeant First Class Eric J. Vidal, the army's top recruiter at this, its most productive office, says business is booming. But few flags fly along 125th, and lots of posters express doubt. "Chickens come home to roost," says one. "The sad truth is that America has killed more African-Americans Than Osama bin Laden Ever Will," reads another.

At the House of Justice, where Al Sharpton is broadcasting his weekly radio show, they rise for the singing of "Lift Every Voice and Sing," the Negro National Anthem, written in 1900 by James Weldon Johnson and his brother. Sharpton's theme this week is the recent deaths of innocent black folks—killed in crossfire, killed for a gold chain—at the hands of other black folks.

"We have been fighting the wrong enemies," he says. "Say that again, slow. Call somebody you know, tell them to turn on the radio, someone you know been fighting the wrong enemy. Somebody in the beauty parlor, come out from under the dryer, you need to hear this. Dry later.

"We've been fighting the wrong enemies," says Sharpton. "Whole communities are turned into the OK Corral."

At the Record Shack, Allan Katatumba, a young man from Uganda who has

Lieutenant Jim Hurley and firefighter Elliot Colon of Engine 36, on 125th Street and MLK Boulevard in East Harlem, sign autographs for passing schoolchildren.

just moved with his wife, a white woman he met while living in Idaho, into an apartment across from Sharpton's headquarters, comes by to offer Shange his support. He calls Shange "Chief."

For hours they argue African politics. Shange has raised money to rebuild a school in his home village and returns frequently with supplies. The poverty back home is beyond American comprehension, he says, but the source of that misery is, in his view, the same as that which threatens his future on MLK—"capitalism."

"We're about to be hanging by our own bootstraps," he says.

We return in October 2002 for a thirty-fifth anniversary celebration of Madhubuti's Third World Press at the Schomburg, up Malcolm X from MLK.

The Reverend Al Sharpton

Among those there to praise Madhubuti is the actor Ossie Davis, who thirty-seven years earlier delivered the eulogy at Malcolm X's funeral. On this day Davis remarks on a puzzle of black life that could serve as an epigram for life along King: "I don't know what God intended by making us so gifted on the one hand and so impecunious on the other. I'm sure He's got something in mind which He'll explain to us later."

In the meantime, Sharpton is preparing to run for president (in January 2003, the day after he files papers to set up a presidential committee and two days after his annual MLK tribute there, the House of Justice burns), Shange is still hanging by a thread, and Franco the Great has painted two new murals on the Apollo side of 125th. One is of King celebrating his birthday. The other depicts an angelic Bill Clinton in a baby blue dashiki holding aloft in either hand images of MLK and Malcolm X. On the building rim above the riot gate bearing the Clinton mural there is, in scrawled script, an advertisement for Puppy's

Leather Outlet. "WOMEN LARGE SIZES," it reads. "Eat What You Want, Then Come See Puppy!!"

And that is where our journey along Martin Luther King ends, directly across Martin Luther King Boulevard in Harlem from the very spot where, but for a sneeze forty-four years before, King's journey would have been cut a decade short, and ours would never have begun.

Chapter 10

Coda:
Back to the Muck

In the fall of 2002, William Asbury, the new postmaster in Belle Glade, Florida, told the city commission that they had to choose whether to call the street that runs east and west past City Hall Avenue E, as it has always been known, or Martin Luther King Jr. Boulevard, as it has also been known since 1990.

Asbury explained that most of the mail being sent to the (whiter) end of the street, east of Main Street, carried an Avenue E address, while most of the mail headed to the (blacker) end, west of Main, bore a Martin Luther King address. That meant a lot of hand sorting, said Asbury, which is costly and slow. In the modern age of postal automation, he said, a street can have only one official name and the commission must decide between MLK and E. And, he pleaded, with all due respect (Asbury is black), if they chose Martin Luther King, could they please make it easier on everyone and shorten it to MLK.

In January the commission, with its black majority, chose Martin Luther

Jerita Marehead at a Jamaican Seventh-day Adventist revival meeting, Belle Glade, Florida

In time for King Day 2003, Willie B. McKenzie of Belle Glade's Public Services Department replaces the old Martin Luther King Boulevard signs with new ones.

King Jr. Boulevard. But they did not oblige Asbury's request that they reduce the street's official name to its initials. On the contrary, they voted to add "Dr." to the street's name.

So on MLK weekend 2003, precisely three years since we began our journey here, we are back in Belle Glade to see the Avenue E signs come down and the new Dr. Martin Luther King Jr. Boulevard signs go up. A perfect ending. Closure.

Or maybe the opposite of closure; maybe a chance to get back on King, to keep going. To not end.

Being back in Belle Glade feels good, like going home. The street seems smaller than we remembered, and less fearsome. The parade doesn't just seem bigger and better, it is. Even the parade route is less constricted, though those lining the route are still almost all black.

Addressing the tight Glades Central band just before the parade begins, the legendary band leader, Willie Pyfrom, in his last year on the job, reminds the young musicians of the meaning of the day: "You were not even born when he died, but you all have heard enough to know this is the most important day for black folks all over America. So don't embarrass yourselves."

We find folks in fine fettle: Lester Finney, Annie Williams, James Leonard, the Millers. Gus Miles, aspiring to be a good Muslim, has sold Tiny's liquors but still has his market a few blocks away. The Reverend J. Richard Harris has launched his candidacy for the March city commission election and campaigns in his idiosyncratic style—calling folks over (they come), quizzing them about their residency and registration, and then, if they pass muster, handing them his leaflets. He looks great. He is driving a blue Lexus (the gift of a godson who plays for the Cleveland Browns). He is wearing a Rolex (the gift of a Tampa Bay

Timica Canty, Glades Central High School marching band

As the parade passes by. Martin Luther King Day, Belle Glade, Florida

Buccaneer). And he is shod in a sweet pair of brown alligator shoes identical to those he admired on a man at Ray Lewis's murder trial on the MLK in Atlanta back in 2000. During the lunch break, the man, who admired Harris's devotion to Lewis, went out and bought Harris his own pair of the same shoes.

After the parade, later in the day, we reconnect with Cartheda Taylor Mann, an English teacher at Glades Central who we met on our first trip. We rendezvous on the roof of the Roof Garden, a residence hotel on King. Off and on in 1950 and 1951, Zora Neale Hurston, seeking refuge after surviving the scandal of a false charge of child molestation in Harlem, lived at the hotel, then nice, now not so. Ten years later Hurston died broke and, for many years afterward, mostly forgotten.

Mann, born in 1949, grew up across the street, behind her family's funeral home, which has since moved up King. When, as a young woman, Mann told her father, W. C. Taylor, she wanted to be a writer, he told her, "The one writer we knew couldn't afford to bury herself when she died." It was not until Mann was in graduate school in African American literature at Boston University and read Hurston's classic, *Their Eyes Were Watching God*, much of it set in Belle Glade, that she realized who that writer was. "That probably was the most exciting week of my life, just learning that and being able to connect the dots to stories from my house," she tells us.

She later learned the story of how a trail-blazing organization—the Glades Inter-Racial Council—founded by her father, a white florist by the name of Sara Lee Creech, and others, would incubate Creech's creation of the Sara Lee doll, hailed as America's first anthropologically correct black doll. Creech enlisted influential patrons, including Eleanor Roosevelt, and the doll, produced by the Ideal Toy Co., appeared in the 1951 Sears, Roebuck and Co. Christmas catalog. Zora Neale Hurston was part of the "color jury" that chose just the right shade

Cartheda Taylor Mann on the roof of the Roof Garden Hotel, where Zora Neale Hurston once lived. Cartheda, who grew up across the street, holds a replica of the Sara Lee doll, for which she modeled as an infant, and whose skin tone Hurston helped choose.

of black for the doll. And, Mann would learn, her own infant face was used as a model for the doll, making her an avatar of black is beautiful before she could even talk.

We are joined on the roof by Donald Neal, an artist. For a while, Mann had a Zora Neale Hurston museum in Belle Glade, and its youth arts program produced a book, illustrated by Neal, about Lawrence Shuler, a businessman who built a bridge in Belle Glade in 1930, but because he was black, the powers-that-be would place his name only under the bridge.

As we talk it dawns on us that we had heard of Neal and tried to make contact with him during our first visit, to no avail. We follow him to his little studio a block up King. The door slams hard behind us. He is a painter and sculptor, and he has created Eve in both mediums, so real they seem divinely inspired. Eve is white because Neal, approaching fifty, is determined not to give the art

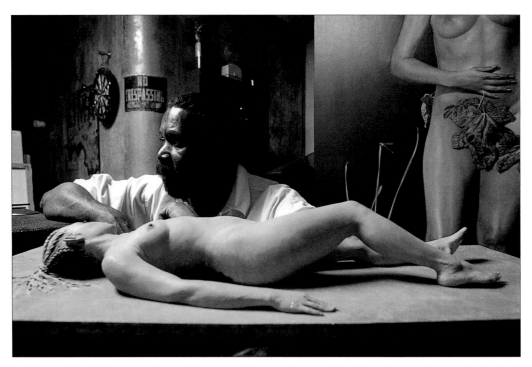

Creator Donald Neal with his sculpture of Eve lying on Adam's tomb

Belle Glade's 2003 Martin Luther King Day Parade ends with an image of King painted on a sheet by Muhammad Lester Finney and hung across the back of a city sanitation truck. It is intended to be evocative of King's support for striking sanitation workers, which in April 1968 brought him to Memphis, where he was assassinated.

world the clues he has seen it use to discount him. If Neal's muse is here in the muck, his market is not, his genius much praised but mostly unrewarded.

At first, we are distressed not to have stumbled upon Neal before the last night of our last trip. We could have missed him altogether. How could we have missed him before? What else did we miss? But there's the rub and the revelation. We, of course, missed so much in our journey along Martin Luther King. What we found was great, and what we didn't—who knows? Our return to Belle Glade persuades us we could keep traveling Kings, even King streets we've already traveled, and it would only get better, deeper, richer.

As Marion Tumbleweed Beach, the seer of Selma, puts it in the parting words of a two-hour telephone conversation the Sunday after our return from Belle Glade: "Good hunting. The end is not the end. We are evolving."

Acknowledgments

This book began as a newspaper series produced by Newhouse News Service. It would never have happened absent the talent, vision, and confidence of Bureau Chief Deborah Howell, Deputy Bureau Chief Linda Fibich, and Director of Photography Toren Beasley. Their enthusiasm matched ours in ways that liberated the undertaking from the ordinary.

We are also indebted to Robert Barnett, the incomparable lawyer and agent, who saw something he liked and sold Random House on the idea.

At Random House, our editor, Melody Guy; her assistant, Danielle Durkin; the book's designer, Mercedes Everett; production editor Janet Wygal; copy editor Susan Brown; and production manager Stacy Rockwood made the creation of this book an absolute pleasure from beginning to end.

Throughout, Bob Kapoor, Ashma Vohra, and J. R. Martin at Duggal New York provided indispensable guidance and film-processing services.

We would also like to thank Derek Alderman, a geographer at East Carolina University, for his outstanding work counting, mapping, and studying Martin Luther King streets across America.

And, most of all, we remain forever grateful to the many remarkable people we met in our travels along Martin Luther King.

J.T. and M.F.

Permissions Acknowledgments

Grateful acknowledgment is made to the following for permission to reprint previously published material:

BROOKS PERMISSIONS: Excerpts from "The Last Quatrain of the Ballad of Emmett Till" and "Chicago, the I Will City" by Gwendolyn Brooks. Reprinted by consent of Brooks Permissions.

HAL LEONARD CORPORATION: Excerpt from "Higher Ground," words and music by Stevie Wonder, copyright © 1973 (renewed 2001) by Jobete Music Co., Inc., and Black Bull Music c/o EMI April Music, Inc. All rights reserved. International Copyright Secured. Used by permission.

PARADISE FREEJAHLOVE (A.K.A. RICHARD MOORE): Excerpt from "I Love Everything About You but You," written by Paradise AKA Richard Moore, President International Black Writers & Artists Local #5, CEO Oakland's World's Fair 2012. Contact paradise@promoteunity.com for books and CDs. Reprinted by permission.

STERLING LORD LITERISTIC: Excerpt from "Why Is We Americans" by Amiri Baraka, copyright by Amiri Baraka. Reprinted by permission of Sterling Lord Literistic.

THIRD WORLD PRESS, INC.: Excerpt from a poem from *Groundwork: New and Selected Poems* by Don L. Lee/Haki R. Madhubuti, copyright © 1996 by Haki Madhubuti. Reprinted by permission of Third World Press, Inc., Chicago, Illinois.

About the Author

JONATHAN TILOVE has covered race for Newhouse News Service since 1991. He is a three-time winner of the National Headliner Award and in 2001 was honored with a lifetime achievement award from Columbia University's Workshops on Journalism, Race & Ethnicity. In 2003 he was the winner of the Freedom Forum/American Society of Newspaper Editors Award for Outstanding Writing on Diversity, and was a finalist for the Scripps Howard Foundation's Ernie Pyle Award, for the newspaper series on which this book is based.

About the Photographer

MICHAEL FALCO is a freelance photographer based in New York City whose work has appeared in *National Geographic, The New York Times*, British *Vogue, W, Harper's Bazaar,* and *Garden Design*. He is the winner of numerous Associated Press photo awards and was a finalist in the 2002 Gordon Parks Photography Competition for one of his *Along Martin Luther King* images. Michael is also a New York City–commissioned Public Artist.

About the Type

The text of this book was set in Janson, a misnamed typeface designed in about 1690 by Nicholas Kis, a Hungarian in Amsterdam. In 1919 the matrices became the property of the Stempel Foundry in Frankfurt. It is an old-style book face of excellent clarity and sharpness. Janson serifs are concave and splayed; the contrast between thick and thin strokes is marked.